HOW TO
TAME YOUR THOUGHTS

Biblical Tools for Overcoming Worry,
Anxiety, Depression, and Negative Thinking

DAVID HART

COPYRIGHT © 2025 BY DAVID HART. ALL RIGHTS RESERVED.

No part of this book may be reproduced, duplicated, or transmitted in any form or by any means, including photocopying, recording, or other electronic or mechanical methods, without prior written permission from the author or publisher, except in the case of brief quotations embodied in critical reviews and certain other non-commercial uses permitted by copyright law.

ISBN: 978-1-716-87087-3

Published by: Sharp Press

TABLE OF CONTENTS

INTRODUCTION 8
CHAPTER 1: THE THOUGHT WARS 11
   Your Mind Under Siege 11
   The Hidden Cost of Untamed Thoughts 13
   Why Traditional Approaches Fall Short 14
   The Promise of Real Change 16
CHAPTER 2: THE SCIENCE BEHIND YOUR THOUGHTS 19
   How Your Brain Creates Reality 19
   Neuroplasticity: Your Brain's Superpower 22
   The Thought-Emotion-Action Connection 26
   Breaking Free from Mental Autopilot 29
CHAPTER 3: GOD'S DESIGN FOR YOUR MIND 34
   Created to Think Like Heaven 34
   Biblical Foundations of Mental Health 37
   The Spirit of Power, Love, and Sound Mind 39
   Reclaiming Your Mental Territory 42
CHAPTER 4: PILLAR ONE - CAPTURE YOUR THOUGHTS 47
   The Art of Mental Awareness 47
      Biblical mental awareness involves several key components: 50
   Recognizing Thought Patterns Before They Take Root 51

Common destructive thought patterns include: 51

The process of early recognition involves several stages: 53

The 5-Second Rule for Thought Intervention 54

Here's how to apply the 5-Second Rule to thought intervention: 56

The 5-Second Rule is particularly effective for common thought-life challenges: 57

Building Your Mental Watchtower 58

Your mental watchtower consists of several key components: 58

Your mental watchtower should be equipped with specific tools: 60

CHAPTER 5: PILLAR TWO - TEST AGAINST TRUTH 63

Scripture as Your Mental Filter 63

Identifying Lies vs. God's Truth 67

The TRUTH Framework for Thought Evaluation 71

T - Test Against Scripture 71

R - Recognize the Results 72

U - Understand the Ultimate Source 73

T - Trust God's Character 74

H - Hold Fast to Hope 74

Creating Your Personal Truth Arsenal 75

CHAPTER 6: PILLAR THREE - REPLACE AND REDIRECT 81

The Power of Intentional Thinking 82

Biblical Meditation Techniques 85

4

Rewiring Your Mental Pathways 90

Thinking Like Jesus in Real Time 94

CHAPTER 7: DEFEATING THE WORRY MONSTER 99

Understanding Anxiety's Grip on Your Mind 99

The Neuroscience of Fear and Faith 104

Practical Strategies for Worry-Free Living............................... 109

Building Unshakeable Peace...114

CHAPTER 8: BREAKING FREE FROM GUILT AND SHAME... 120

The Difference Between Conviction and Condemnation 121

Healing from Past Mistakes 125

The Freedom of Forgiveness 129

Walking in Your New Identity 134

CHAPTER 9: OVERCOMING DEPRESSION AND DESPAIR 139

When Your Mind Feels Hijacked.. 140

Hope as a Powerful Weapon 143

Creating Mental Momentum... 147

Finding Light in the Darkness... 151

CHAPTER 10: SILENCING THE INNER CRITIC 156

The Voice of Self-Condemnation.. 157

Replacing Negative Self-Talk 161

Building Healthy Self-Worth 165

Speaking Life Over Your Future 170

CHAPTER 11: THE POWER OF GRATITUDE AND PRAISE 176

Rewiring Your Brain for Joy 177
Scientific Benefits of Thanksgiving 181
Creating Daily Gratitude Practices 186
When Praise Becomes Your Default 191

CHAPTER 12: PROTECTING YOUR MENTAL ENVIRONMENT 198

Guarding the Gates of Your Mind 199
Media, Relationships, and Mental Health 203
Creating Healthy Boundaries 208
Building a Life-Giving Support System 213

CHAPTER 13: THE DISCIPLINE OF MENTAL RENEWAL 219

Making Thought Management a Lifestyle 220
Daily Practices for Mental Health 224
Handling Setbacks and Relapses 229
Growing Stronger Through Challenges 234

CHAPTER 14: THINKING LIKE JESUS IN EVERY SITUATION 241

Developing Christ-Centered Perspectives 242
Responding vs. Reacting 246
Love as Your Mental Operating System 250
Walking in Divine Wisdom 255

CHAPTER 15: HELPING OTHERS TAME THEIR THOUGHTS 260

Becoming a Minister of Mental Health 261
Supporting Loved Ones in Their Journey 266

Creating Healthy Family Thought Patterns 271
Building Communities of Mental Wellness 276
CHAPTER 16: YOUR NEW MIND, YOUR NEW LIFE 282
Celebrating Your Transformation... 283
Maintaining Long-Term Mental Health................................... 287
Continuing to Grow and Evolve 291
Living as an Overcomer... 295
CONCLUSION **300**

INTRODUCTION

The war for your mind began the moment you woke up this morning. Perhaps it started with that familiar knot in your stomach as your thoughts immediately spiraled to today's worries—the upcoming meeting, the unpaid bills, the relationship conflict you've been avoiding. Maybe it was the whisper of shame reminding you of yesterday's failures, or the heavy blanket of depression telling you that nothing will ever change. For many of us, our minds have become battlegrounds where anxiety, worry, and negative thinking wage daily warfare against our peace, our purpose, and our potential.

You are not alone in this struggle. Millions of people around the world find themselves trapped in cycles of destructive thinking, feeling powerless to break free from the mental quicksand that threatens to pull them under. The statistics are staggering: anxiety disorders affect over 40 million adults in the United States alone, while depression impacts more than 17 million Americans each year. But these numbers only tell part of the story. Behind each statistic is a real person—perhaps someone just like you—who goes to bed each night hoping tomorrow's thoughts will be different, only to wake up to the same mental chaos.

Here's what I want you to know: the thoughts that have characterized your past do not have to define your future. The God who created your magnificent brain has not abandoned you to fight this battle alone. In fact, He's provided you with everything you need—both in His Word and through the incredible discoveries of modern neuroscience—to completely transform your thought life. You don't have to remain stuck in patterns of worry, anxiety, depression, or negative thinking that have held you captive for months, years, or even decades.

This book is your roadmap to mental freedom. It's not just another self-help guide filled with positive thinking platitudes or empty promises. Instead, it's a comprehensive, biblically-grounded approach that combines the timeless wisdom of Scripture with cutting-edge insights from neuroscience and psychology. You'll discover that God's design for your mind is far more powerful than you ever imagined, and that He's equipped you with practical tools to take every thought captive and make it obedient to Christ.

Throughout these pages, you'll learn the three foundational pillars of thought mastery that can revolutionize your mental landscape: how to capture your thoughts before they capture you, how to test every mental message against the unshakeable truth of God's Word, and how to replace destructive thinking patterns with thoughts that align with heaven's perspective. You'll discover why the apostle Paul's instruction to "be transformed by the renewal of your mind" isn't just spiritual advice—it's a neurologically sound strategy for rewiring your brain for health, hope, and wholeness.

But this isn't just about managing your thoughts; it's about experiencing the abundant life Jesus promised. It's about waking up each morning with peace instead of panic, facing challenges with confidence rather than fear, and living from a place of mental strength rather than emotional chaos. It's about becoming the person God designed you to be—someone with "a sound mind" who can think clearly, love deeply, and walk in the power and purpose He's placed within you.

Whether you're struggling with persistent worry that keeps you awake at night, anxiety that makes simple tasks feel overwhelming, depression that clouds every decision, or negative thinking patterns that have become your mental default, this book offers hope. Real, lasting, transformational hope. Because if God can resurrect the dead, He can certainly resurrect your thought life. If He can part seas, He can part the clouds of confusion in your mind. If He can turn water into wine, He can turn your mental chaos into clarity, your anxiety into peace, and your despair into unshakeable joy.

The journey ahead won't always be easy—real transformation rarely is. But it will be worth it. As you apply these biblical tools and scientific insights to your daily thought life, you'll begin to experience the mental freedom you've been longing for. You'll discover that you're not a victim of your thoughts; you're the victor over them. And you'll learn that with God as your helper, no mental stronghold is too strong to be demolished, no negative pattern too entrenched to be changed, and no thought life too broken to be beautifully restored.

Your mind is not your enemy—it's waiting to become your greatest ally in living the life God has called you to live. Let's begin this journey together, one thought at a time.

CHAPTER 1: THE THOUGHT WARS

The battlefield is invisible, but the casualties are everywhere. Walk through any office, school hallway, or church sanctuary, and you'll encounter the walking wounded—people whose minds have become war zones where destructive thoughts rain down like artillery shells, leaving craters of anxiety, depression, and despair. They smile and nod, go through the motions of daily life, but inside, they're fighting for their mental survival against an enemy that never sleeps, never retreats, and never shows mercy.

This is the reality of the thought wars—the daily mental combat that millions of people face but rarely discuss openly. Unlike physical wounds that draw sympathy and immediate attention, the injuries inflicted by untamed thoughts remain hidden beneath the surface, festering in silence while slowly poisoning every aspect of life. The enemy knows that if he can win the battle for your mind, he's already won the war for your life. Your thoughts become the gateway through which victory or defeat enters your reality, shaping not just how you feel, but who you become and what you achieve.

Your Mind Under Siege

Every morning, 57.8 million Americans wake up to an invisible enemy that has already begun its assault. The NIH estimates that over 57 million Americans live with a mental illness, and for many of them, the first conscious moments of each day are hijacked by an internal dialogue of worry, fear, and negative anticipation. This isn't simply a case of "waking up on the wrong side of the bed"—it's evidence of a sophisticated warfare being waged in the most important battlefield of human existence: the mind.

The statistics paint a sobering picture of this mental siege. Approximately 19.1% of adults have had an anxiety disorder within the last year, while 21 million adults reported having at least one episode of major depression, which is roughly 8.3 percent of the U.S. adult population. But these numbers only scratch the surface of a deeper crisis. Recent research reveals that 43% of adults say they feel more anxious than they did the previous year, up from 37% in 2023 and 32% in 2022, indicating that the siege is not only widespread but intensifying.

The enemy's strategy is brilliantly designed to exploit the very architecture of our brains. Neuroscientist Rick Hanson describes this vulnerability perfectly: "Your brain is like Velcro for negative experiences and Teflon for positive ones." This isn't a character flaw or personal weakness—it's an evolutionary feature called negativity bias that once helped our ancestors survive on the African savanna but now leaves us defenseless against the psychological threats of modern life.

What makes this siege particularly devastating is its stealth nature. Unlike physical attacks that announce themselves with pain and visible wounds, the assault on our minds often goes undetected until significant damage has already occurred. Negative thinking patterns can be a formidable obstacle, holding us back from reaching our full potential, creating what researchers call "repetitive negative thinking" (RNT)—a cycle of destructive thoughts that captures an important transdiagnostic factor that predisposes to a maladaptive stress response and contributes to diverse psychiatric disorders.

Consider the current landscape of mental warfare that surrounds us daily. Adults are particularly anxious about current events (70%) — especially the economy (77%), the 2024 U.S. election (73%), and gun violence (69%). The constant bombardment of negative news, social media comparisons, financial pressures, and global uncertainties creates what psychologists term "ambient anxiety"—a low-level but persistent state of mental agitation that slowly erodes our psychological defenses.

The Hidden Cost of Untamed Thoughts

The price tag for mental chaos doesn't appear on any monthly statement, yet it extracts a toll more devastating than any financial debt. Depression and anxiety disorders cost the global economy $1 trillion in lost productivity each year, while serious mental illness costs the country more than $190 billion in lost earnings every year. But these numbers represent only the tip of an iceberg whose true dimensions extend far deeper into human experience.

Recent groundbreaking research involving 20,000 anxiety disorder patients revealed that negativity bias can cause brain abnormalities, reduced blood flow in key regions, and higher levels of depression, memory issues and poor stress regulation. Research conducted at King's College London reveals that prolonged negative thinking diminishes the brain's capacity to think, reason, and form memories. This isn't metaphorical damage—it's measurable, physical alteration of brain tissue that shows up on brain scans.

The cardiovascular system pays an equally devastating price. People with depression have a 40% higher risk of developing cardiovascular and metabolic diseases than the general population. The brain, it turns out, doesn't distinguish between facts and fantasies when we color events with negativity. Instead, it assumes that a real danger exists in the world and unleashes potentially destructive brain chemicals, like cortisol.

Perhaps most shocking is the impact on longevity. Those with a severe mental illness have a life span 10 to 25 years shorter than the general population. Chronic negative thinking patterns literally steal decades from our lives by accelerating aging at the cellular level and compromising immune function.

The cognitive costs are equally devastating. Researchers say repetitive negative thinking can increase your risk for developing dementia, with studies showing that participants who exhibited repetitive negative thinking had more cognitive decline and problems with memory. They were also more likely than participants who didn't have repetitive negative thinking patterns to have amyloid and tau deposits in their brains—the same protein deposits that characterize Alzheimer's disease.

Why Traditional Approaches Fall Short

The landscape of mental health treatment is littered with good intentions and partial solutions. Almost 6 in 10 people with mental illness get no treatment or medication. In 2024, an estimated 57.8 million adults (19% of the country) had a mental illness, but only 43% received any kind of mental health care. But the problem isn't just access—it's the fundamental inadequacy of approaches that treat symptoms while ignoring deeper spiritual and neurological realities.

Modern psychiatry's first response is often pharmaceutical intervention—a chemical solution to what is frequently a spiritual and psychological problem. While medications can provide crucial stabilization, they represent what Dallas Willard called "the tyranny of the urgent," treating symptoms while leaving root causes untouched. The fundamental flaw is the reductionist approach assuming complex spiritual realities can be addressed by adjusting neurotransmitter levels.

Traditional psychotherapy, while valuable, often fails because it operates from humanistic assumptions without acknowledging spiritual dimensions. Cognitive Behavioral Therapy can teach people to recognize distorted thinking, but it cannot provide the divine truth that sets captives free. The limitation becomes apparent when people understand their thinking is distorted but feel powerless to change it.

The positive thinking movement promises we can think our way to happiness, but it often amounts to psychological makeup applied to spiritual wounds. Instead you have to embed optimism in your brain through the power of "non-negative thinking." Forced positivity asks people to deny legitimate concerns and often increases psychological distress.

Perhaps most significantly, traditional approaches are fragmented. Mental health care has been divided into competing specialties—

psychiatrists, psychologists, life coaches, and spiritual counselors—rarely addressing the whole person. This compartmentalized approach reflects broader fragmentation where spiritual, psychological, and physical realities are treated as separate domains rather than interconnected aspects of unified human experience.

The Promise of Real Change

After decades of disappointment, many have resigned themselves to managing mental suffering rather than expecting genuine transformation. But what if this resignation isn't necessary? The promise of real change isn't based on human optimism—it's grounded in the reality of who God is and what modern neuroscience reveals about the brain's capacity for transformation.

The most exciting discovery in neuroscience is that the brain is remarkably plastic, meaning it has the ability to reorganize and adapt its neural pathways in response to experience and learning. This concept, known as neuroplasticity, is key to understanding how we can overcome negative thinking patterns and cultivate a more positive mindset.

Where previous generations believed mental patterns were largely fixed by adulthood, we now know the brain continues reshaping itself throughout life based on focused attention. In the words of early neuroscientist Donald Hebb, "neurons that fire together, wire together." Every time you choose God's truth over anxious thoughts, you're rewiring neural pathways to make peace more automatic.

Long before neuroscientists discovered neuroplasticity, God revealed mental transformation through His Word. Romans 12:2 instructs believers to "be transformed by the renewal of your mind"—assuming such transformation is possible and expected. The Greek word metamorphoo implies complete change of form, like a butterfly's metamorphosis.

If you repetitiously focus on the word "peace," saying it aloud or silently, you will begin to experience a sense of peacefulness in yourself and in others close to you. The thalamus will respond to this incoming message of peace, and it will relay the information to the rest of the brain. Pleasure chemicals like dopamine will be released, the reward system of your brain will be stimulated, anxieties and doubts will fade away, and your entire body will relax.

Research confirms that this kind of exercise will increase the thickness of your neocortex and shrink the size of your amygdala, the flight-or-fight mechanism in your brain. Biblical practices don't just provide comfort—they create measurable brain changes supporting long-term mental health.

The promise rests on three foundational pillars combining biblical principles with neurological realities: capturing thoughts before they spiral, testing every mental message against Scripture's truth, and replacing destructive patterns with thoughts aligned with heaven's perspective.

Real change is possible because if God can resurrect the dead, He can resurrect your thought life. If He can part seas, He can part

17

confusion in your mind. The same neuroplasticity that allows negative thoughts to create decline can be harnessed for cognitive renewal. Your mind wasn't designed to be a battlefield—it was designed to be a fortress of peace, creativity, and divine connection.

The war for your mind is real, but victory isn't just possible—it's promised. The question isn't whether you can win; it's whether you're ready to stop being a casualty and start being a victor.

CHAPTER 2: THE SCIENCE BEHIND YOUR THOUGHTS

Every thought you think is a symphony of electrical activity cascading through billions of neural networks, creating the reality you experience moment by moment. What seems like the simple act of "thinking" is actually one of the most complex and fascinating processes in the known universe. Your brain doesn't just passively receive information from the world around you—it actively constructs your reality, shapes your emotions, and determines your actions through mechanisms so sophisticated that scientists are only beginning to understand their full scope and power.

This chapter will take you on a journey through the cutting-edge discoveries of neuroscience that reveal how your thoughts literally reshape your brain, influence your emotions, and direct your behavior. You'll discover that your brain possesses an almost supernatural ability to rewire itself throughout your entire life, and you'll learn how to harness this power to break free from destructive thought patterns that have held you captive. Understanding the science behind your thoughts isn't just academic curiosity—it's the foundation for experiencing the mental freedom that God intended for you.

How Your Brain Creates Reality

The most astonishing revelation of modern neuroscience is that the reality you experience isn't actually "reality" at all—it's a sophisticated construction project happening inside your skull. The deeper truth is that perception is never a direct window onto an objective reality. All our perceptions are active constructions, brain-based best guesses at the nature of a world that is forever obscured behind a sensory veil.

Your brain is constantly engaged in what neuroscientists call "predictive processing"—a remarkable system where the brain is attempting to figure out what is out there in the world (or in here, in the body) by continually making and updating best guesses about the causes of its sensory inputs. This means that every moment of your conscious experience is actually your brain's best interpretation of incoming sensory data, filtered through your past experiences, beliefs, and expectations.

Consider something as simple as the color red. The mug really does seem to be red: its redness seems as real as its roundness and its solidity. These features of my experience seem to be truly existent properties of the world, detected by our senses and revealed to our mind through the complex mechanisms of perception. Yet we have known since Isaac Newton that colors do not exist out there in the world. Instead they are cooked up by the brain from mixtures of different wavelengths of colorless electromagnetic radiation.

This reveals a profound truth: your brain is not a passive recording device but an active reality-creation machine. Our perception of reality is not an exact representation of the objective truth but rather a combination of sensory inputs and the brain's interpretation of these signals. This interpretation is influenced by past experiences and is often predictive, with the brain creating categories of similar instances to anticipate future events.

The implications for your thought life are staggering. If your brain is constantly constructing your reality based on predictions and interpretations, then the thoughts you habitually think literally shape the world you experience. When anxiety dominates your thinking, your brain constructs a reality filled with threats and dangers. When gratitude fills your mind, your brain builds a reality abundant with blessings and opportunities.

This construction process extends far beyond simple perception. The brain's quest for stability and its pursuit of energy efficiency means that your mind seeks patterns and shortcuts to make sense of information quickly. Your brain creates categories and associations that influence not just what you see, but how you interpret everything that happens to you.

The revolutionary insight is that "If we are successful, then we'll be able to more fully understand reality, the truth", but the reality we experience is not fixed or unchangeable. Since your brain constructs your experienced reality through its interpretive processes, changing your thought patterns can literally change your experienced reality.

"The exhibit gives the visitor an idea of how their brains make assumptions about the world around us. We have the feeling that we see a perfect replica of everything, like a photograph, but our brain makes continuous choices about what to pay attention to and thus determines what enters our consciousness". This selective attention process means that what you focus your thoughts on consistently literally shapes what your brain allows into your conscious awareness.

The practical application is profound: when you begin to understand that your brain is actively constructing your reality based on the thoughts you feed it, you realize you have far more power over your experience than you ever imagined. The anxious person isn't experiencing a more dangerous world—they're experiencing a world constructed by an anxious brain. The depressed person isn't living in a more hopeless reality—they're experiencing reality through the filter of depressive thinking patterns.

This doesn't mean that external circumstances don't matter, but it does mean that your brain's interpretation of those circumstances—shaped by your thought patterns—has enormous influence over your actual lived experience. When you change your thoughts, you don't just change your mood; you change the reality your brain constructs for you moment by moment.

Understanding this process empowers you to take responsibility for your mental experience in a way that's both scientifically grounded and spiritually profound. Your thoughts aren't just fleeting mental events—they're the building blocks of your experienced reality.

Neuroplasticity: Your Brain's Superpower

Perhaps the most revolutionary discovery in neuroscience history is the realization that your brain possesses an almost miraculous ability to rewire and reshape itself throughout your entire life. Neuroplasticity, the brain's capacity to reorganize itself by forming new neural connections, is central to modern neuroscience. Once believed to occur only during early development, research now shows that plasticity continues throughout the lifespan, supporting learning, memory, and recovery from injury or disease.

This discovery completely overturns the old belief that adult brains were essentially fixed and unchangeable. Neuroplasticity, also known as neural plasticity or brain plasticity, is a process that involves adaptive structural and functional changes to the brain. A good definition is "the ability of the nervous system to change its activity in response to intrinsic or extrinsic stimuli by reorganizing its structure, functions, or connections".

The mechanism behind this superpower is elegantly simple yet profoundly powerful. Donald Hebb described an important process for learning in the brain, known as Hebbian learning (1949), summed up by the phrase, "neurons that fire together wire together." Put simply, when two or more neurons respond or fire at the same time (i.e., from some thought, action, or event in the environment) the connection or synapse between them is strengthened, leading to a stronger association.

This means that every thought you think, every emotion you experience, and every action you take literally changes your brain's physical structure. Learning and memory are necessarily closely linked. You cannot learn something without storing it in some form of memory for use in the future, either for recall as new knowledge or improvement in skills. When you repeatedly focus on anxious thoughts, you're strengthening neural pathways that make anxiety your brain's default response. When you consistently practice gratitude, you're building neural highways that make thankfulness more automatic.

Recent research has revealed that neuroplasticity operates through multiple mechanisms. Understanding the mechanisms and principles of neuroplasticity offers insightful knowledge of the dynamic nature of the brain and makes it possible to consider various therapeutic approaches for treating neurological illnesses and brain rehabilitation. These mechanisms include synaptic plasticity (changes in the strength of connections between neurons), structural plasticity (physical changes in brain anatomy), and functional reorganization (reassignment of brain functions to different areas).

The research on neuroplasticity and mental health is particularly encouraging. Increasing evidence demonstrates that neuroplasticity, a fundamental mechanism of neuronal adaptation, is disrupted in mood disorders and in animal models of stress. Here we provide an overview of the evidence that chronic stress, which can precipitate or exacerbate depression, disrupts neuroplasticity, while antidepressant treatment produces opposing effects and can enhance neuroplasticity.

This means that the same neuroplasticity that allows negative thought patterns to become entrenched also provides the mechanism for creating positive change. Neuroplasticity plays a crucial role in developing and maintaining brain function, including learning and memory, as well as in recovery from brain injury and adaptation to environmental changes.

Modern technology is revealing new ways to harness neuroplasticity for mental transformation. By combining VR and BCI, researchers can stimulate specific brain regions, trigger neurochemical changes, and influence cognitive functions such as memory, perception, and motor skills. While these high-tech approaches are promising, the most powerful tool for directing neuroplasticity remains something you have access to right now: your attention.

Sensory skills and the ability to understand our surroundings depend on the activity of the brain, which enables us to perceive and process stimuli that come from the outside world. But you have tremendous control over what stimuli you expose your brain to and what you pay attention to consistently.

The practical implications are profound. Every time you choose to focus on Scripture instead of worry, you're rewiring your brain for peace. Every time you practice gratitude instead of complaint, you're strengthening neural pathways for joy. Every time you reject negative self-talk and speak truth over your life, you're literally reshaping your brain's architecture.

Everybody has a different brain, which is influenced by genetics, age, the type of injury, and environmental circumstances. Therefore, it is essential to create tailored strategies that consider these elements to maximize the efficacy of therapies based on neuroplasticity. This means that your journey of mental transformation will be unique to you, but the underlying principle remains the same: consistent, focused attention on truth-based thinking will create measurable changes in your brain.

The hope this provides is immense. No matter how long you've struggled with negative thinking patterns, no matter how deeply entrenched your mental habits seem to be, your brain retains the capacity to change. Neuroplasticity is your brain's superpower, and understanding how to direct it purposefully is the key to experiencing the mental transformation that God promises in His Word.

The Thought-Emotion-Action Connection

One of the most practical discoveries in neuroscience is understanding how thoughts, emotions, and actions are intricately connected in continuous feedback loops that shape your entire life experience. Moods and other, more transient emotional states tend to encourage congruent thoughts and actions (e.g., Lerner et al., 2015), a process that is necessarily mediated by enduring changes in brain activity and connectivity.

This isn't just a philosophical concept—it's a measurable neurological reality. Emotions are thought to be related to activity in brain areas that direct our attention, motivate our behavior, and help us make decisions about our environment. Your brain contains sophisticated networks that constantly integrate cognitive and emotional information to produce your moment-by-moment experience.

The pathway typically works like this: your thoughts trigger emotional responses through activation of brain regions like the amygdala and limbic system. The amygdalae are involved in detecting and learning which parts of our surroundings are important and have emotional significance. These emotional responses then influence your actions and behaviors, which in turn reinforce the original thought patterns, creating self-perpetuating cycles.

Understanding this connection is crucial because it reveals why simply trying to change behavior without addressing underlying thought patterns is often ineffective. Emotion feeling is a phase of neurobiological activity, the key component of emotions and emotion-cognition interactions. When your thoughts consistently generate negative emotions, those emotions drive actions that often reinforce the negative thinking, creating what psychologists call "vicious cycles."

For example, when you think "I'm not good enough" (thought), this generates feelings of shame and inadequacy (emotion), which leads to avoidance behaviors or self-sabotage (action), which then provides "evidence" that supports the original thought of inadequacy. The cycle becomes self-reinforcing and self-fulfilling.

The good news is that this connection works in reverse as well. Emotion utilization is the harnessing of an emotion's inherently adaptive emotion motivation/feeling component in constructive affective-cognitive processes and actions. When you deliberately choose truth-based thoughts, they generate positive emotions that motivate constructive actions, which then reinforce the positive thought patterns.

Modern research has revealed the specific brain mechanisms involved in this process. control is engaged when there is uncertainty about the optimal course of action (e.g., probabilistic learning), when potential actions are associated with the possibility of error or punishment, or when there is competition between alternative courses of action. This explains why changing thought patterns requires conscious effort—you're literally rewiring neural networks that have operated automatically.

Emotion regulation is a critical life skill that can facilitate learning and improve educational outcomes. Learning to interrupt negative thought-emotion-action cycles and replace them with positive ones isn't just beneficial for mental health—it's essential for optimal brain function and life success.

The prefrontal cortex plays a crucial role in this process. The prefrontal cortex is the front of the brain, behind the forehead and above the eyes. It plays a role in regulating emotion and behavior by anticipating consequences. The prefrontal cortex also plays an important role in delayed gratification by maintaining emotions over time and organizing behavior toward specific goals.

This means you have neurological equipment specifically designed to interrupt automatic thought-emotion-action cycles and consciously choose more constructive patterns. success in emotionally motivated behaviors is associated with integrating numerous physical sensations, thoughts, and ongoing contextual and affective experiences and promptly producing the most appropriate responses.

Practically, this research validates the biblical principle of taking thoughts captive. When you notice a negative thought arising, you can use your prefrontal cortex to evaluate it, choose a truth-based response, and intentionally generate emotions and actions aligned with that truth. Over time, this rewires your brain's default responses.

Health behavior includes at least health mindsets, decision-making, and actions that contribute to health outcomes across the lifespan. Understanding the thought-emotion-action connection empowers you to approach mental health as an integrated whole, addressing thoughts, feelings, and behaviors as interconnected aspects of your overall well-being.

The key insight is that you don't have to be a victim of automatic thought-emotion-action cycles. With understanding and practice, you can learn to intercept negative patterns and consciously choose responses that align with truth, generating positive emotions and constructive actions that build mental health rather than destroy it.

Breaking Free from Mental Autopilot

Your brain operates much like a sophisticated autopilot system, running background programs that control the majority of your daily thoughts, emotions, and behaviors without your conscious awareness. The default mode network is an area of the brain that acts as an autopilot whenever your mind wanders or you disconnect from your surroundings in a state of relaxing self-absorption.

This system, called the Default Mode Network (DMN), was one of the most significant discoveries in modern neuroscience. Marcus

Raichle, MD, first coined the term for this fascinating brain system in 2001 when he found that certain parts of the brain lit up on brain scans while the brain was not engaged in specific tasks. The DMN includes key brain regions like Medial prefrontal cortex, located behind your forehead [and] Posterior cingulate cortex, situated near the middle of your brain.

These brain regions activate when you reminisce about your past, imagine the future, or consider other people's perspectives. Think of the DMN as the human brain's autopilot. It's at work in the background while your mind wanders. While this system serves important functions for memory consolidation and self-reflection, it can become problematic when it's dominated by negative thought patterns.

The research reveals concerning connections between DMN dysfunction and mental health issues. Depression: In people experiencing clinical depression, the DMN can be overly active when they're resting, according to research. This means their brain might be getting stuck on sad or negative thoughts. This type of rumination is like a record player skipping and repeating the same gloomy song.

Similarly, Anxiety: In people who often feel anxious, the DMN may be overactivated. This hyperconnectivity can make them worry too much about the future or regret things from the past. It's as if the brain is constantly running "what if" scenarios that increase anxiety disorders.

The autopilot problem becomes particularly challenging when you consider how much of your mental life operates below conscious awareness. A set of brain regions, collectively known as the default mode network (DMN), may play a crucial role in such "autopilot" behavior. Concurrent with mental processes that require rigorous computation and control, a series of automated decisions and actions govern our daily lives, providing efficient and adaptive responses to environmental demands.

However, recent research has revealed something hopeful: the DMN also has positive functions that can be harnessed for mental health. These findings indicate a memory-based "autopilot role" for the default mode network, which may have important implications for our current understanding of healthy and adaptive brain processing. When functioning properly, the DMN helps with creative thinking, problem-solving, and integrating experiences into coherent narratives.

The key insight is learning how to influence your mental autopilot rather than being controlled by it. The discovery of the default mode network (DMN) has revolutionized our understanding of the workings of the human brain, particularly in understanding how we can consciously influence what happens during those automatic mental processes.

One of the most effective ways to retrain your mental autopilot is through mindfulness and meditation practices. In a study of meditators, some were more adept at meditating and others more neophyte. The more experienced meditators had much less activity in the default mode network, they were much better than the neophyte in curtailing mind wandering.

Meditation – Structural changes in areas of the DMN such as the temporoparietal junction, posterior cingulate cortex, and precuneus have been found in meditation practitioners. There is reduced activation and reduced functional connectivity of the DMN in long-term practitioners. This research demonstrates that you can literally rewire your mental autopilot through consistent spiritual practices.

The practical application involves developing what neuroscientists call "meta-cognitive awareness"—the ability to observe your own thought processes. The brain often switches freely between focused attention and divergent thinking, and the Default Mode Network (DMN) is activated during brain rest. By becoming aware of when your mind shifts into autopilot mode, you can consciously redirect it toward more constructive patterns.

Biblical meditation serves as a particularly powerful tool for retraining the DMN. When you consistently fill your mental autopilot with Scripture, worship, and truth-based thinking, you're literally rewiring the background programs that run in your mind throughout the day. the DMN integrates and broadcasts memory, language, and semantic representations to create a coherent "internal narrative" reflecting our individual experiences. This narrative is central to the construction of a sense of self.

The goal isn't to eliminate your mental autopilot—it serves important functions for creativity and memory processing. rest promotes learning which continues when people rest their brain. A scientific brain break will make learning easier and more enjoyable. Instead, the goal is to ensure that your autopilot is programmed with truth rather than lies, hope rather than despair, and faith rather than fear.

Breaking free from destructive mental autopilot patterns requires both understanding the science and applying biblical principles consistently. As you become more aware of your default mental processes and intentionally redirect them toward truth, you'll discover that your unconscious mind becomes an ally in mental transformation rather than an enemy working against your peace and joy.

CHAPTER 3: GOD'S DESIGN FOR YOUR MIND

Your mind was never intended to be a chaotic battlefield where negative thoughts wage war against your peace and purpose. From the very beginning, God designed your mind to be a sanctuary of divine connection, a place where His truth reigns supreme and His Spirit brings clarity, peace, and power. Understanding God's original design for your mind isn't just theological curiosity—it's the foundation for reclaiming the mental freedom that has always been your birthright as His child.

This chapter reveals the profound truth that your struggles with anxiety, depression, and negative thinking aren't just psychological issues to be managed—they're spiritual realities that require both divine intervention and your active participation in God's restoration process. You'll discover that the same God who spoke creation into existence has spoken specific promises over your mind, and that these promises provide both the blueprint and the power for complete mental transformation.

Created to Think Like Heaven

When God created humanity in His image, He didn't just give us bodies that reflected His nature—He designed our minds to operate according to heavenly principles and perspectives. Underlying these principles is the fundamental view Scripture presents of humans as integrated beings—with body, mind and spirit working in harmony. The apostle Paul wrote to the church in Thessalonica, "May the God of peace Himself sanctify you completely; and may your whole spirit, soul, and body be preserved blameless at the coming of our Lord Jesus Christ" (1 Thessalonians 5:23).

This integration means that your mind was designed to function in perfect harmony with God's Spirit, not in opposition to it. Our thoughts have the power to shape the way we perceive ourselves and influence how we interact with others. Throughout the Bible, we see verse after verse reminding us of the importance of our thoughts and why we need to allow the Holy Spirit to renew our minds.

The original design for human thinking involved what we might call "heaven's perspective"—seeing reality through God's eyes rather than through the distorted lens of fallen human reasoning. For those who live according to the flesh set their minds on the things of the flesh, but those who live according to the Spirit, the things of the Spirit. For to be carnally minded is death, but to be spiritually minded is life and peace.

This heavenly thinking pattern is characterized by several key elements. First, it operates from truth rather than deception. God's design for your mind includes built-in discernment that recognizes truth and rejects lies. Second, it functions from love rather than fear. "Peace I leave with you; My peace I give you; not as the world gives do I give to you. Do not let your heart be troubled and do not be afraid." Third, it processes information through hope rather than despair, always seeing possibilities for redemption and restoration.

When you think like heaven, you naturally align with God's perspective on your circumstances, your identity, and your future.

"...for you are a chosen people. You are royal priests, a holy nation, God's very own possession. As a result, you can show others the goodness of God, for He called you out of the darkness into His wonderful light." This is how God sees you, and when your mind operates according to His design, this is how you see yourself.

The Fall disrupted this design, introducing patterns of thinking that oppose God's truth. In Genesis 3, we see sin enter the world, which causes creation to long for restoration [Romans 8:22]. When sin entered the world, there were physical effects on the body and soul. However, the original blueprint remains intact, and through Christ's redemptive work, God is restoring your mind to its intended function.

Paul takes us deeper than Peter here. He penetrates beneath the "futile mind" and the "darkened understanding" and the willful "ignorance" and says that it is all rooted in "the hardness of their heart." Here is the deepest disease, infecting everything else. Our mental suppression of liberating truth is rooted in our hardness of heart.

The good news is that God has provided both the means and the power to restore your mind to its original design. Ultimately, God wants me to be transformed to be like his Son, Jesus. Jesus did not engage in the type of mental machinations that I've described—he was totally focused on the will of the Father. Because that was true of him, it will increasingly be true of me…and someday, that work in me will be complete.

Creating a mindset aligned with heaven's perspective involves regularly asking yourself: "How does God see this situation? What is God's truth about this circumstance? How would Jesus think about this challenge?" When you consistently return your thoughts to these heavenly perspectives, you're not just thinking positively—you're thinking according to your original design.

Biblical Foundations of Mental Health

Scripture provides a comprehensive framework for understanding mental health that goes far beyond managing symptoms to addressing the root spiritual and psychological foundations of human flourishing. This perspective parallels contemporary mental health approaches that consider humans holistically, integrating biological, psychological and social factors in human development and health. We are at our best when body, mind and spirit work in harmony; we also thrive when we're in harmony with others.

The biblical foundation begins with understanding that mental health challenges aren't signs of spiritual weakness or lack of faith. And just like our physical health is not guaranteed, neither is our mental health. The mind, like the body, can become ill. Charles Spurgeon once said, "The mind can descend far lower than the body, for in it there are bottomless pits. The flesh can bear only a certain number of wounds and no more, but the soul can bleed in ten thousand ways."

Scripture acknowledges the reality of mental and emotional struggles among God's people. We have a biblical example in Elijah, whose mental health suffered during his conflict with Queen

Jezebel. The psalms are filled with expressions of depression, anxiety, and emotional turmoil, yet they consistently point toward God as the source of healing and restoration.

Our "heroes of the Bible" face moments of struggle directly related to their mental health. We see moments where their mental health suffered as they battled through things like exhaustion or moments of despair. The Psalms also are filled with heartache and broken spirit cries to God. But time and time again, we see God restoring, encouraging, and renewing the hearts and minds of His people.

The Bible's approach to mental health is fundamentally relational. Both the Bible and modern psychology point to secure relationships as the foundation of good mental health. When Jesus was asked to name the most important commandment, He responded, "'You shall love the Lord your God with all your heart, with all your soul, and with all your mind.' This is the first and greatest commandment".

Mental renewal is presented as both a divine gift and a human responsibility. Therefore I urge you, brethren, by the mercies of God, to present your bodies a living and holy sacrifice, acceptable to God, which is your spiritual service of worship. And do not be conformed to this world, but be transformed by the renewing of your mind, so that you may prove what the will of God is, that which is good and acceptable and perfect.

The process involves several key elements. First, recognizing the source of destructive thoughts. I know who the enemy is, and I also know the only One who can defeat him. Recognize the enemy, and fight him with God's power and with Scriptural truth. Second, actively replacing lies with truth. When negativity or doubt try to take up space in our minds—we must counter those thoughts with God's Word and speak His truth to every lie.

Scripture also emphasizes the importance of community in mental health. God never meant for us to go through life alone. In fact, Ecclesiastes 4:9-10 (NIV) says, "Two are better than one, because they have a good return for their labor: If either of them falls down, one can help the other up. But pity anyone who falls and has no one to help them up."

The biblical foundation also includes practical wisdom for daily mental health practices. Take your anxieties to Jesus in prayer. Let him carry them. Write them down and throw them into the trash can. When anxious thoughts creep into your mind, say out loud, "I throw that off and give it to God."

Most importantly, Scripture grounds mental health in the unchanging character and promises of God. When our mental health is compromised, we often feel alone and isolated. We can second-guess ourselves and everything we believe in. This scripture on mental health reminds us that God is always God, no matter what we may feel or what tricks our brain may be trying to play on us.

The Spirit of Power, Love, and Sound Mind

Perhaps no verse captures God's design for your mental state more powerfully than 2 Timothy 1:7: "For God has not given us a spirit of fear, but of power, love, and sound mind." This declaration reveals three foundational elements that God has embedded in your spiritual DNA, providing the framework for healthy thinking and emotional stability.

The opening phrase of this verse may explain why Paul dwells so much on concepts such as bravery and spiritual strength when writing to Timothy. It's possible this represented a spiritual weakness which Paul was helping Timothy to overcome. Perhaps Timothy was content in his role of serving alongside Paul and did not prefer to be the outspoken leader of a large movement of Christians.

The first element—power—refers to supernatural ability that comes from God's Spirit within you. This is the Resurrection power on which we stand, the reality of placing our faith in Jesus, who has the power to conquer sin as proven by his ability to conquer death. This power isn't just for dramatic miracles; it's the daily strength to choose truth over lies, hope over despair, and faith over fear.

by which the minds of Christ's servants are fortified against reproaches and persecutions for his sake, and are strengthened to resist Satan's temptations, to endure hardness as good soldiers of Christ, to quit themselves like men, in opposition to false teachers, and to do the will and work of God.

The second element—love—provides the motivation and context for healthy thinking. Love is a fruit of the Spirit (Galatians 5:23), without which all we do is as annoying and obnoxious as walking around banging a cymbal (I Corinthians 13). This word for love is, of course, "agape" – the plural, by the way, is "love feast" (remember Jude?) It's not just a mindset; it's an action.

When your thoughts are motivated by God's love—both your understanding of His love for you and your love for Him and others—they naturally become more constructive and life-giving. Love-motivated thinking asks different questions: "How can I serve?" rather than "What's in it for me?" "How can I understand?" rather than "How can I judge?" "How can I build up?" rather than "How can I tear down?"

The third element—sound mind—is perhaps the most directly relevant to mental health. Finally, the verse mentions the spirit of a sound mind. This refers to a mind that is balanced, clear, and disciplined. It is a mind that is not overtaken by fear or irrational thoughts but is grounded in the truth of God's word. Through the Holy Spirit, believers are able to have a sound mind that enables them to think rationally, make wise decisions, and exercise self-control.

A better word is "self-discipline" or "self-control", another fruit of the Spirit. This is essential first of all so that we do not disqualify ourselves from the race God has called and prepared us to run (1 Corinthians 9:27). It's what helps us live with gospel integrity.

The Greek word used here for "sound mind" is "sophronismos," which describes a person who is sensibly minded and balanced, who has his life under control. The Amplified Version reads, "calm and well-balanced mind and discipline and self-control."

This doesn't mean you'll never experience difficult emotions or challenging thoughts. Rather, it means you have the spiritual equipment to process them in healthy ways. The point is that timidity or fear is not an abnormal human emotion, but it should not be one's prevailing mindset, for we have all, like Timothy, been given the abundant provision of grace in God's "power and love and sound mind."

These three elements work together synergistically. Power without love becomes harsh and destructive. Love without sound thinking becomes sentimental and ineffective. Sound thinking without power and love becomes cold and academic. But when all three operate together, they create the mental environment that God intended for your flourishing.

When those endowments are all present, marvelous results occur. These are not natural endowments. We are not born with them, and they cannot be learned in a classroom or developed from experience. They are not the result of heritage or environment or instruction. But all believers possess these marvelous, God-given endowments: power, to be effective in His service; love, to have the right attitude toward Him and others; and discipline, to focus and apply every part of our lives according to His will.

Reclaiming Your Mental Territory

Your mind is territory, and every territory in this spiritual war must be intentionally claimed and defended. Our minds become a battlefield as we wrestle with our thinking. Often, we don't take hold of our thoughts. Instead, we allow them to run wild causing overwhelm. Because of our mental strongholds, battles are won or lost in our minds before we make a single move.

Understanding this territorial nature of mental warfare is crucial for lasting freedom. If we let these thoughts flow unchecked, not recognizing their source, we begin to come into agreement with them. Our thinking develops certain patterns, or mindsets — things we believe to be true, although they are not. When that happens, the enemy of our souls is on the way to establishing a "stronghold" — a fortress within our head, from which he can disseminate even more lies.

A stronghold is essentially mental territory that has been occupied by the enemy through repeated agreement with lies, fears, or destructive thought patterns. A stronghold is an area in which we are held in bondage, due to a certain way of thinking. These are caused by mind binding spirits. Satan establishes these to interrupt our destiny as Christians.

A strong hold properly means a fastness, a fortress, or strong fortification. The bible refers to David's hiding places as strongholds [1 Sam 22:4-5; 24:22] It is used in this scripture however, to symbolize the various obstacles resembling a fortress that exists in our minds.

The process of reclaiming mental territory follows the strategy outlined in 2 Corinthians 10:3-6. "For though we walk in the flesh, we do not war after the flesh. For the weapons of our warfare are not carnal, but mighty through God to the pulling down of strongholds, casting down imaginations, and every high thing that exalteth itself against the knowledge of God, and bringing into captivity every thought to the obedience of Christ."

First, you must recognize that this is spiritual warfare, not just psychological struggle. Spiritual warfare consists of struggling against evil forces in our minds. The Bible is clear that this is not a battle which is fought on a physical plane at all, but rather a spiritual one. Ephesians 6:12 (HCSB) For our battle is not against flesh and blood, but against the rulers, against the authorities, against the world powers of this darkness, against the spiritual forces of evil in the heavens.

Second, you must use spiritual weapons, not human strategies alone. We are in a spiritual battle, and we must fight with spiritual weapons. God has given us His Word as our main line of defense against the lies of the enemy. These weapons include prayer, Scripture, worship, declaration of truth, and the authority you have in Christ's name.

Third, you must actively "pull down" strongholds rather than simply trying to ignore them. Pulling down and putting away take effort on our part. This involves identifying the lies you've believed, repenting of agreement with those lies, and declaring God's truth over those areas of your mind.

Fourth, you must "take captive" every thought. Take captive every thought. The Greek word aichmalōtizō there means "to control, to conquer, to bring into submission." We take captive. We make it submit. Every thought obedient to Christ. Make it obedient. Hupakøe means "to bring into submission, to bring under control."

If we bring something into captivity, we hold it as if it is a prisoner of war. POWs are not excused, coddled, or treated lightly. This means you don't have to accept every thought that comes to your mind as true or valid. You have the authority to interrogate thoughts, test them against Scripture, and reject those that don't align with God's truth.

Fifth, you must occupy reclaimed territory with truth. We should not leave those territories of former evil influence unoccupied, however. The Holy Spirit wants to help us replace our old mindsets with His. We can ask Him to build up strongholds of the Lord in place of the enemy's strongholds which were there before. The erecting of God's strongholds comes through absorbing, confessing, and actively believing the Word of God.

The key to maintaining your mental freedom is understanding that Changing our behavior doesn't change the source of our problems. We have to renew our minds. We have to get to the root of the issue. If we don't pull up a weed from it's root, then it will just grow right back in a matter of time. If we don't learn to think differently, nothing will ever change. Those strongholds will start to rise up again.

Practical steps for reclaiming mental territory include: daily meditation on Scripture, regular prayer for mental protection and clarity, accountability relationships with mature believers, and consistently speaking God's truth over your life and circumstances. Remember, The more we know His Word and get it deep down on the inside of us, the more we will enjoy freedom in every area of our lives.

Your mind was never meant to be occupied territory. It was designed to be a sanctuary where God's Spirit dwells, where His truth reigns, and where His peace rules. The battle for your mental territory is real, but so is your authority in Christ to reclaim and defend what belongs to you.

CHAPTER 4: PILLAR ONE - CAPTURE YOUR THOUGHTS

The first step in any successful military campaign is reconnaissance—gathering intelligence about the enemy's position, movements, and tactics before engaging in battle. In the war for your mind, this intelligence-gathering phase involves developing the skill of mental awareness: the ability to observe your own thinking patterns, recognize the source of your thoughts, and intercept destructive mental patterns before they establish strongholds in your consciousness.

Most people live their entire lives unconscious of their thought processes, allowing an endless stream of mental chatter to flow unchecked through their minds. They mistake every thought that arises as "their" thought, never realizing that many of these mental messages originate from sources that oppose their wellbeing and God's purposes for their lives. Learning to capture your thoughts is like installing a sophisticated early warning system in your mind—it alerts you to potential threats before they can cause damage and gives you the power to choose your response rather than simply reacting automatically.

The Art of Mental Awareness

Mental awareness, also known as metacognition, is an awareness of one's thought processes and an understanding of the patterns behind them. The term comes from the root word meta, meaning "beyond", or "on top of". Metacognition can take many forms, such as reflecting on one's ways of thinking, and knowing when and how oneself and others use particular strategies for problem-solving.

This capacity for self-observation is what separates humans from all other creatures. The heart of metacognition is students becoming aware of the subjective experience that underpins learning, monitoring it, understanding it, and regulating/adapting it to maximise learning. This means shifting the students' awareness to a deeper, more introspective, self-reflective level. In the context of thought management, metacognition enables you to step outside your thinking and observe it objectively, like watching a movie of your own mental processes.

The biblical foundation for this practice is found throughout Scripture. David prayed, "Search me, God, and know my heart; test me and know my anxious thoughts" (Psalm 139:23-24). This wasn't just a passive prayer—it was an active invitation for God to help him develop awareness of his own mental and emotional patterns. Similarly, Paul instructs believers to examine themselves: "Examine yourselves to see whether you are in the faith; test yourselves" (2 Corinthians 13:5).

Developing mental awareness requires understanding that metacognition refers to the ability to observe and analyze our own cognitive processes. It's the act of stepping back from our thoughts and observing them from an outsider's perspective. This mental skill involves monitoring, evaluating, and regulating our thinking, often with the aim of improving our problem-solving abilities and decision-making.

The neuroscience behind mental awareness reveals fascinating insights. Recent advances in neuroscience have revealed that metacognition corresponds with certain brain activities: Prefrontal

Cortex Activation: This region, responsible for higher-order functions, plays a pivotal role in metacognition. It helps in organizing thoughts, regulating behavior, and overseeing cognitive processes. Enhanced Neural Connectivity: People with higher metacognitive abilities often exhibit more robust connections between different brain regions, facilitating efficient mental processing.

The practice begins with what researchers call "mindful meta-awareness." These are a receptive or mindful awareness, with openness to whatever "comes to mind in the moment", which has been shown to create a state of flexibility in self-regulation enabling an individual to profoundly shift out of habitual ways of adapting and reacting. This involves cultivating a non-reactive stance toward your thoughts—observing them without immediately judging, believing, or acting upon them.

The involvement of metacognition in mindfulness is already acknowledged in recent mindfulness models. The focus of the current paper is on how mindfulness may be seen to involve a particular subcategory of metacognitive feeling referred to as fringe consciousness. This "fringe consciousness" represents those subtle mental experiences that occur at the edges of your awareness—the slight tension before a negative thought, the faint unease that precedes anxiety, or the gentle pull toward destructive mental patterns.

Biblical mental awareness involves several key components:

Observer Self vs. Thinking Self: Learning to distinguish between the part of you that thinks and the part of you that observes thinking. The observer self remains calm and detached, while the thinking self generates the constant stream of mental activity.

Thought Labeling: Developing the ability to categorize thoughts as they arise. Is this thought true or false? Helpful or harmful? From God, self, or the enemy? The Bible echoes this concept in 2 Corinthians 10:5, "We demolish arguments and every pretension that sets itself up against the knowledge of God, and we take captive every thought to make it obedient to Christ".

Present-Moment Anchoring: Mindfulness refers to a mental state achieved by focusing one's awareness on the present moment, while calmly acknowledging and accepting one's feelings, thoughts, and bodily sensations. This prevents you from getting lost in past regrets or future anxieties.

Non-Judgmental Observation: Watching your thoughts without immediately condemning yourself for having them. Remember, you are not responsible for every thought that enters your mind, but you are responsible for what you do with those thoughts once you become aware of them.

The goal isn't to achieve a thoughtless mind—that's neither possible nor desirable. Instead, the goal is to develop what scripture calls "a sound mind" (2 Timothy 1:7), where you have conscious authority over your mental processes rather than being unconsciously controlled by them.

Recognizing Thought Patterns Before They Take Root

Just as a skilled gardener can spot weeds when they're still seedlings, developing the ability to recognize destructive thought patterns in their earliest stages is crucial for maintaining mental health. Pattern recognition occurs when information from the environment is received and entered into short-term memory, causing automatic activation of a specific content of long-term memory. In the context of mental health, this means your brain automatically connects current situations with stored memories and established thought patterns.

Negative thought patterns are often automatic, distorted, unhelpful, believable, and intrusive. These thoughts can lead to detrimental behaviors and hinder personal growth if left unaddressed. Recognizing specific patterns aids in reframing thoughts and improving mental well-being.

Common destructive thought patterns include:

Catastrophizing: Immediately jumping to worst-case scenarios. When you're five minutes late, your mind creates an entire story about losing your job, becoming homeless, and dying alone.

All-or-Nothing Thinking: Viewing situations in black and white terms with no middle ground. "If I'm not perfect, I'm a total failure."

Mind Reading: Assuming you know what others are thinking about you, usually assuming the worst. "She didn't text me back immediately; she must hate me."

Fortune Telling: Predicting negative outcomes with no evidence. "This presentation will be a disaster."

Emotional Reasoning: Believing that because you feel something, it must be true. "I feel worthless, therefore I am worthless."

The key to interrupting these patterns is catching them in what researchers call the "recognition phase"—the moment when a pattern is triggered but before it fully develops. Recognizing patterns allows anticipation and prediction of what is to come. Making the connection between memories and information perceived is a step in pattern recognition called identification.

Biblical insight reveals that destructive thought patterns often begin with specific spiritual and emotional triggers:

Pride: Thoughts that focus on your superiority or inferiority compared to others

Fear: Anxious projections about future scenarios

Anger: Rehearsing offenses and planning retaliation

Shame: Self-condemnation and identity attacks

Unbelief: Questioning God's goodness, power, or promises

To effectively recognize negative thought patterns, individuals can use various strategies such as: Journaling: Keeping a thought log allows individuals to track their negative thoughts and identify triggers. Mindful Reflection: Practicing mindfulness helps individuals become more aware of their thought processes without judgment. Talking it Out: Discussing feelings and thoughts with others can provide clarity and perspective. Check for Cognitive Distortions: Regularly questioning thoughts against the cognitive distortions list can highlight inaccuracies.

The process of early recognition involves several stages:

Trigger Awareness: Learning to identify the external circumstances, internal sensations, or emotional states that typically precede destructive thinking patterns. This might be certain people, places, times of day, physical sensations, or memories.

Mental Posture Recognition: Noticing the subtle shift in your mental stance when you begin moving toward negative thinking. This often feels like a mental "bracing" or a slight tension in your thought process.

Narrative Interruption: Recognizing the moment when your mind begins constructing a negative story about your circumstances. Instead of allowing the story to develop, you can pause and ask, "Is this narrative true? Is it helpful? Does it align with God's perspective?"

Energy Shift Detection: Paying attention to how different thought patterns affect your emotional and physical energy. Destructive patterns typically create a sense of heaviness, agitation, or depletion, while constructive patterns generate peace, hope, and strength.

Developing this recognition ability requires patience and practice. Pattern recognition requires repetition of experience. The more consistently you practice observing your thought patterns, the more quickly you'll recognize them in their early stages.

The 5-Second Rule for Thought Intervention

When you recognize a destructive thought pattern beginning to form, you have a critical window of opportunity to intervene before it gains momentum. Research by Mel Robbins has identified this window as approximately five seconds—the brief moment between recognizing an impulse and your brain either acting on it or talking you out of it.

Every human being has a five-second window might even be shorter for you. You have about a five-second window in which you can move from idea to action before your brain kicks into full gear and sabotages any change in behavior. Because remember, your brain is wired to stop you from doing things that are uncomfortable or uncertain or scary.

The 5-Second Rule for thought intervention works by understanding the neuroscience of hesitation. What none of us realize is that when you hesitate just that moment, that micro-moment, that small hesitation it sends a stress signal to your brain. When you hesitate to take control of a negative thought pattern, your brain interprets this as a signal that the situation might be dangerous, activating your body's stress response and making it harder to think clearly.

The rule is deceptively simple: The 5 Second Rule is simple. If you have the instinct to act on a goal, you must physically move within 5 seconds or your brain will kill it. The moment you feel an instinct or a desire to act on a goal or a commitment, use the Rule.

Applied to thought management, this means that when you recognize a destructive thought pattern beginning, you have five seconds to take physical action to interrupt it before your brain's automatic systems take over and make intervention much more difficult.

The neuroscience behind this approach is compelling. Robbins explains that hesitation triggers the brain's amygdala, which governs fear and avoidance. The 5 Second Rule disrupts this process, redirecting focus to action. Neuroscience supports this mechanism; by engaging the prefrontal cortex, individuals can override their natural tendency to avoid discomfort or risk.

Here's how to apply the 5-Second Rule to thought intervention:

Count Down: When you notice a destructive thought pattern beginning, immediately count backwards: 5-4-3-2-1. The counting serves multiple purposes: it interrupts the thought pattern, focuses your attention, and activates your prefrontal cortex.

Physical Movement: Physical movement is key. Just so you understand, this doesn't mean you have to jump up and start doing squats. All you need to do is move in the direction of your instinct. If you do not take physical action WITHIN 5 SECONDS, your brain will kill the instinct. This might involve standing up, taking a deep breath, opening your Bible, or making a specific gesture.

Immediate Replacement: Use the physical movement to immediately replace the destructive thought with a specific truth from Scripture or a predetermined positive declaration. The key is having these replacement thoughts ready in advance.

Action Commitment: Follow the intervention with a small, immediate action that reinforces your decision to reject the destructive pattern. This might involve praying, texting an encouraging message to someone, or doing a brief physical exercise.

The biblical foundation for rapid intervention is found in James 4:7: "Submit yourselves therefore to God. Resist the devil, and he will flee from you." The word "resist" in Greek (anthistemi) means to take a stand against, to oppose actively. It's not a passive response but an immediate, decisive action.

Research from neuroscientist Antonio Damasio's research further supports Robbins' approach. He found that emotions drive up to 95% of decisions. By treating feelings as suggestions rather than absolute barriers, individuals can act despite discomfort or doubt. This is crucial for thought intervention because destructive thoughts often come with strong emotional components that can overwhelm rational decision-making if not addressed quickly.

The 5-Second Rule is particularly effective for common thought-life challenges:

Worry Spirals: The moment you notice your mind beginning to create catastrophic scenarios about the future, count down and physically redirect your attention to a specific Scripture about God's provision.

Self-Condemnation: When you catch your inner critic beginning its attack, immediately interrupt with the countdown and speak a truth about your identity in Christ.

Temptation Thoughts: The instant you recognize a tempting thought, use the rule to physically remove yourself from the situation or engage in a predetermined accountability action.

Remember, the simple reason we often don't act at all is that we "don't feel like it." To solve this problem, Mel suggests we should let professional athletes inspire us. They consider feelings suggestions, rather than absolutes, which allows them to override them – for example with the 5 Second Rule – and push further towards their goal.

Building Your Mental Watchtower

In ancient times, cities built watchtowers at strategic locations to provide early warning of approaching enemies. Watchmen would maintain constant vigilance, scanning the horizon for any signs of threat. In the spiritual realm, building a mental watchtower involves establishing consistent practices and perspectives that help you maintain awareness of your thought life and respond quickly to mental threats.

The biblical concept of watchfulness is central to spiritual warfare. Jesus repeatedly emphasized the importance of staying alert: "Watch and pray so that you will not fall into temptation. The spirit is willing, but the flesh is weak" (Matthew 26:41). The word "watch" (gregoreo in Greek) means to stay awake, to be vigilant, to guard against surprise attack.

Your mental watchtower consists of several key components:

Daily Mental Inventory: Self-regulation requires metacognition by looking at one's awareness of their learning and planning further learning methodology. Attentive metacognition is a salient feature of good self-regulated learners, but does not guarantee automatic application. This involves setting aside time each day to review your thought patterns, identify triggers, and assess your mental state.

Scripture Meditation: Regular, focused engagement with God's Word provides the foundational truth against which all other thoughts are measured. Romans 12:2 says, "Do not conform to the pattern of this world but be transformed by the renewing of your mind." Christian Cognitive Behavioral Therapy integrates these principles by helping clients recognize and modify distorted thinking patterns to foster healthier emotions and behaviors.

Environmental Awareness: Understanding how your physical environment, relationships, media consumption, and daily rhythms affect your thought patterns. Individuals need to regulate their thoughts about the strategy they are using and adjust it based on the situation to which the strategy is being applied.

Trigger Mapping: Creating a detailed awareness of the specific circumstances, emotions, physical sensations, and relational dynamics that typically precede your most challenging thought patterns.

Accountability Systems: Establishing relationships with mature believers who can help you maintain perspective and provide external wisdom when your own judgment becomes clouded.

Regular Spiritual Disciplines: Prayer, worship, fellowship, and service create a spiritual environment that naturally supports healthy thinking patterns and provides strength for mental battles.

Building your watchtower also involves developing what researchers call "metacognitive strategies." It has been proposed that MABIs incorporate a set of interrelated practices to cultivate a present-moment awareness and mindful attention, train metacognitive skills such as decentering and distancing, with aim to facilitate an accepting and compassionate stance toward one's experience rather than attempting to avoid or otherwise control it.

The process of decentering is particularly important—this involves learning to step back from your thoughts and observe them objectively rather than being emotionally fused with them. When a thought arises, instead of immediately accepting it as true or reacting emotionally, you learn to observe it with curiosity: "That's an interesting thought. Where did it come from? Is it true? Is it helpful? How does it align with God's perspective?"

Your mental watchtower should be equipped with specific tools:

Truth Arsenal: A collection of Bible verses and biblical truths that directly counter your most common destructive thought patterns.

Pattern Recognition Checklist: A mental or written list of your personal thought pattern triggers and early warning signs.

Intervention Strategies: Predetermined responses to different types of mental attacks, including the 5-Second Rule applications, physical movements, prayer declarations, and accountability contacts.

Recovery Protocols: Plans for what to do when you've already fallen into destructive thinking patterns, including repentance, truth declaration, and restoration practices.

Support Network: Clear understanding of who to contact for prayer, encouragement, or accountability when facing particularly intense mental battles.

Remember that building a mental watchtower is an ongoing process, not a one-time construction project. Metacognition is 'stable' in that learners' initial decisions derive from the pertinent facts about their cognition through years of learning experience. Simultaneously, it is also 'situated' in the sense that it depends on learners' familiarity with the task, motivation, emotion, and so forth.

The ultimate goal of your mental watchtower is not to live in a state of hypervigilance or anxiety about your thoughts, but to develop the kind of relaxed awareness that comes from confidence in God's protection and your own ability to recognize and respond to mental threats. Like a skilled watchman who can distinguish between a threatening army and a traveling merchant caravan, you'll learn to quickly assess the spiritual significance of your thoughts and respond appropriately.

As you consistently practice capturing your thoughts through mental awareness, pattern recognition, quick intervention, and vigilant watchfulness, you'll discover that what once seemed like an overwhelming battle for your mind becomes increasingly manageable. The enemy's tactics become predictable, your responses become automatic, and your mind becomes the peaceful sanctuary God intended it to be.

CHAPTER 5: PILLAR TWO - TEST AGAINST TRUTH

The mind is a battlefield, and every day, thousands of thoughts compete for your attention, your belief, and ultimately, your allegiance. Some thoughts arrive like trusted friends, whispering encouragement and hope. Others sneak in like thieves in the night, carrying lies that feel so convincing you barely notice they've stolen your peace. The question isn't whether you'll have thoughts—that's as inevitable as breathing. The question is: how will you determine which thoughts deserve your trust and which ones deserve to be shown the door?

This is where the second pillar of thought management becomes absolutely critical: testing your thoughts against truth. Just as a jeweler uses a touchstone to distinguish genuine gold from fool's gold, we need a reliable standard to separate truth from deception in our mental landscape. Without this filter, we're vulnerable to believing anything that sounds reasonable, feels familiar, or arrives with emotional intensity. But when we learn to test our thoughts against the unchanging truth of God's Word, we develop the spiritual discernment to recognize which mental messages lead to life and which ones lead to destruction. This isn't about positive thinking or mental gymnastics—it's about aligning our minds with reality as God defines it.

Scripture as Your Mental Filter

Modern psychology recognizes that our thoughts, emotions, and behaviors are interconnected, with cognitive patterns often determining our emotional state and subsequent actions. However, while secular cognitive-behavioral approaches focus on replacing unhelpful thoughts with helpful ones, biblical thought management goes deeper by replacing lies with God's truth. Scripture serves as the ultimate mental filter because it represents the mind of God himself—the one who created our brains and understands exactly how they were designed to function.

When we speak of Scripture as a mental filter, we're acknowledging that God's Word possesses unique qualities that make it supremely qualified to evaluate our thoughts. The Bible presents truth as "conformity to reality and opposition to lies and errors," with Hebrew and New Testament texts consistently drawing clear contrasts between truth and falsehood. This isn't subjective truth that changes with cultural trends or personal preferences—this is objective truth that corresponds to ultimate reality.

The apostle Paul understood this filtering process when he wrote in Romans 12:2, "Do not be conformed to this world, but be transformed by the renewal of your mind, that by testing you may discern what is the will of God, what is good and acceptable and perfect." The Greek word for "testing" here is *dokimazo*, which refers to the process of examining something to prove its authenticity—like testing metals to determine their purity. This denotes a two-step process: 1) considering the available evidence and 2) accepting the truth of whatever the reliable evidence shows.

Scripture functions as our mental filter in several crucial ways. First, it provides objective standards that exist outside our subjective experiences and emotions. When anxiety whispers, "You're going to fail," we can test that thought against Philippians 4:13: "I can do all things through him who strengthens me." The thought doesn't automatically disappear, but it loses its power to control us because we've measured it against a higher authority.

Second, Scripture offers comprehensive truth that addresses every area of human experience. Whether you're struggling with fear, guilt, relationships, purpose, or identity, God's Word provides specific truth that speaks directly to your situation. This isn't about proof-texting or taking verses out of context—it's about understanding the consistent message of Scripture regarding God's character, his promises, and his design for human flourishing.

Third, Scripture provides supernatural power to transform our thinking. Hebrews 4:12 reminds us that "the word of God is alive and active. Sharper than any double-edged sword". This isn't merely inspirational literature—it's living truth that penetrates our minds and hearts with divine power. When we filter our thoughts through Scripture, we're not just engaging in mental exercise; we're inviting God himself to renew our minds through his revealed truth.

The filtering process requires both knowledge and practice. You can't filter thoughts through Scripture you don't know, which is why regular Bible study and memorization are essential. But knowledge alone isn't sufficient—you must develop the habit of consciously bringing your thoughts into contact with God's Word. This means pausing when destructive thoughts arise and asking, "What does God say about this? How does his truth address this particular lie or fear or doubt?"

Consider how Jesus himself modeled this practice during his temptation in the wilderness. Each time Satan presented a lie or half-truth, Jesus responded with Scripture: "It is written..." He didn't argue with the temptations or try to reason them away through positive thinking. He countered lies with the authoritative truth of God's Word, demonstrating that Scripture is our most reliable weapon against deception.

The mental filtering process also requires understanding the difference between thoughts and truth. Thoughts are mental events—they come and go, often influenced by circumstances, emotions, physical state, or spiritual attack. Truth, however, is constant and unchanging. Biblical truth is authoritative, exclusive, objective, knowable, and revealed to us for our eternal good. When thoughts contradict Scripture, we don't need to believe them simply because they're loud, persistent, or emotionally convincing.

This filtering system becomes increasingly important in our current cultural moment, where progressive ideas encourage individuals to "live their truth" and pursue whatever feels right to them. But feelings are notoriously unreliable guides to truth. Truth is not determined by how we feel—truth is a statement or belief that lines up with reality. Scripture provides that reality check, offering us truth that transcends our subjective experiences and anchors us in God's perspective.

Developing Scripture as your mental filter is a lifelong process that grows stronger with practice. Start by identifying the most common lies or destructive thought patterns in your life, then search Scripture for truth that directly addresses these areas. Write down specific verses, memorize them, and practice bringing them to mind when the lies surface. Over time, this filtering process becomes more automatic, creating what psychologists call "cognitive restructuring" but what the Bible simply calls having the mind of Christ.

Identifying Lies vs. God's Truth

The battle for your mind is fundamentally a battle between truth and lies, and your enemy is a master deceiver. Jesus identified Satan as "the father of lies" who "speaks his native language" when he lies. Understanding how to distinguish between lies and God's truth isn't just a helpful life skill—it's essential spiritual warfare that determines whether you'll live in freedom or bondage.

Lies often masquerade as truth by containing just enough accuracy to seem believable. They typically appeal to our fears, insecurities, past failures, or current circumstances. The most dangerous lies are those that sound reasonable and align with how we're feeling in the moment. When you're exhausted from a difficult season, the lie "God doesn't care about you" might feel true because your emotions are running low. When you've failed repeatedly in an area, the lie "You'll never change" might seem logical based on your track record.

Satan's lies generally fall into several categories, each designed to undermine your relationship with God and your identity as his beloved child. The first category involves lies about God's character: "God is disappointed in you," "God is withholding good things from you," "God's love is conditional on your performance." These lies attack the foundation of faith by distorting who God really is.

The second category involves lies about your identity: "You're worthless," "You're beyond redemption," "You're not really saved," "You're a failure." These identity lies are particularly destructive because they contradict the fundamental truth that you are fearfully and wonderfully made, chosen by God, and declared worthy through Christ's sacrifice.

The third category involves lies about your circumstances: "This situation will never change," "You're trapped," "There's no hope," "God has abandoned you." These lies take temporary or difficult circumstances and declare them permanent, removing hope and faith from the equation.

The fourth category involves lies about your future: "You'll always struggle with this," "You're destined to repeat your parents' mistakes," "God can't use someone like you." These lies steal vision and purpose by convincing you that change is impossible and God's plans are limited.

In contrast, God's truth consistently reflects his character and his heart toward you. Biblical truth demonstrates internal coherence—it doesn't contradict itself or present God as capricious or unreliable. God's truth always leads to freedom, hope, love, and spiritual growth, even when it includes conviction or calls for repentance.

God's truth about his character remains constant: He is loving, faithful, good, sovereign, present, and committed to your ultimate good. His love isn't based on your performance but on his unchanging nature. His plans for you are good, even when circumstances are difficult. His power is sufficient for every situation you'll face.

God's truth about your identity is equally consistent: You are loved unconditionally, chosen purposefully, forgiven completely, and equipped supernaturally. Your worth isn't determined by your achievements, your mistakes, or other people's opinions—it's established by God's declaration over your life. You are his workmanship, created for good works that he prepared in advance.

God's truth about your circumstances acknowledges difficulty without declaring defeat. Scripture never promises that life will be easy, but it consistently promises that God will be with you, that he can work all things together for good, and that present sufferings cannot compare to the glory that will be revealed. Circumstances are temporary; God's truth is eternal.

One of the most reliable ways to distinguish lies from truth is by examining the fruit they produce in your life. John Mark Comer notes that "ideas have power only when we believe them". Lies consistently produce fear, discouragement, isolation, hopelessness, condemnation, and spiritual paralysis. Truth produces peace, hope, connection, faith, conviction that leads to repentance, and spiritual growth.

Another distinguishing factor is the source and tone of the message. Lies often arrive with urgency, condemnation, and absolutes that allow for no exceptions or hope. They frequently begin with "always" or "never" statements: "You always mess up," "You'll never change," "Nobody cares about you." Truth, while sometimes challenging, arrives with hope, grace, and possibilities for growth and change.

God's truth also aligns with the overall message of Scripture. In religiously integrated cognitive therapy, automatic thoughts are identified and then changed using religious values, teachings, and beliefs. Any "truth" that contradicts the clear teaching of Scripture or undermines the gospel message should be rejected as deception.

The Holy Spirit plays a crucial role in helping believers distinguish truth from lies. Jesus promised that the Spirit would guide us into all truth, and 1 John 4:6 speaks of recognizing "the Spirit of truth and the spirit of falsehood". As you grow in your relationship with God, you'll develop spiritual discernment that helps you recognize the difference between God's voice and the enemy's deceptions.

Learning to identify lies versus truth requires practice and intentionality. Start by paying attention to thoughts that produce fear, shame, hopelessness, or distance from God. Ask yourself: Does this align with what Scripture teaches about God's character? Does this contradict what God has said about my identity in Christ? Does this message lead me toward God or away from him? Is this consistent with the gospel of grace?

When you identify a lie, don't just dismiss it—replace it with corresponding truth from Scripture. This process of replacement is crucial because simply removing lies leaves a vacuum that new lies can fill. But when you replace lies with truth, you're building a foundation of biblical thinking that becomes increasingly resistant to deception.

The TRUTH Framework for Thought Evaluation

Developing a systematic approach to evaluating your thoughts prevents you from being overwhelmed when mental storms arise. The TRUTH framework provides five essential questions to help you quickly and accurately assess whether a thought aligns with God's Word or represents enemy deception. This framework isn't just theoretical—it's a practical tool you can use in real-time to maintain mental and spiritual clarity.

T - Test Against Scripture

The first step in evaluating any thought is to ask: What does Scripture say about this? This isn't about finding a verse to support what you want to believe, but honestly examining whether your thought aligns with the clear teaching of God's Word. Truth claims must pass the test of internal coherence or logical consistency—they must be free of contradictions within their own principles, premises, and conclusions.

If you're thinking, "I'm worthless," test this against Isaiah 43:4: "You are precious in my eyes, and honored, and I love you." If you're thinking, "God has abandoned me," test this against Hebrews 13:5: "I will never leave you nor forsake you." If you're thinking, "I can't be forgiven for what I've done," test this against 1 John 1:9: "If we confess our sins, he is faithful and just to forgive us our sins and to cleanse us from all unrighteousness."

This testing requires familiarity with Scripture, which is why regular Bible reading and memorization are so important. You can't test thoughts against truth you don't know. But as you grow in biblical knowledge, you'll find it increasingly easy to recognize thoughts that contradict God's revealed truth.

R - Recognize the Results

The second question asks: What fruit does this thought produce in my life? Lies consistently produce negativity, fear, and spiritual darkness, while truth leads to freedom, hope, and spiritual growth. This isn't about positive thinking—it's about recognizing that God's truth consistently produces godly character and spiritual fruit.

Thoughts that lead you toward prayer, worship, obedience, love, and faith are likely aligned with truth. Thoughts that lead you toward isolation, despair, rebellion, hatred, and unbelief are likely rooted in deception. Pay attention to the emotional and spiritual trajectory of your thoughts. Do they draw you closer to God or push you away from him?

This evaluation helps you distinguish between conviction and condemnation. The Holy Spirit's conviction leads to repentance, hope, and restoration. Satan's condemnation leads to shame, despair, and spiritual paralysis. Conviction says, "You sinned, but there's forgiveness available." Condemnation says, "You're a terrible person who will never change."

U - Understand the Ultimate Source

The third question examines: Where is this thought ultimately coming from? All lies come from the devil, while truth originates from God. This doesn't mean every negative thought is a direct demonic attack—sometimes lies come from our own flesh, past experiences, or worldly thinking. But ultimately, anything that contradicts God's truth has its source in the kingdom of darkness.

Thoughts that exalt God's character, align with his Word, and promote spiritual growth come from God. Thoughts that diminish God's character, contradict his Word, and hinder spiritual growth come from the enemy. Sometimes the source isn't immediately obvious, which is why you need the other elements of this framework.

Understanding the source helps you respond appropriately. Thoughts from God should be embraced and obeyed. Thoughts from the enemy should be rejected and replaced with truth. This understanding also removes personal condemnation—you're not a bad person for having deceptive thoughts; you're simply recognizing enemy infiltration that needs to be addressed.

T - Trust God's Character

The fourth question asks: Does this thought align with what I know about God's character? God is consistently portrayed in Scripture as loving, faithful, good, sovereign, merciful, and committed to our ultimate good. Any thought that portrays God as cruel, unreliable, limited, or working against your best interests contradicts his revealed character.

God "cannot lie" and "cannot deny himself" or assert what is false. This means that thoughts portraying God as inconsistent, deceptive, or unreliable are automatically false. God's character provides a reliable benchmark for evaluating thoughts about his intentions toward you.

When facing difficult circumstances, lies often attack God's character: "If God really loved you, this wouldn't be happening," or "God is punishing you for your past sins." These thoughts contradict the clear biblical revelation of God's love, grace, and redemptive purposes. Trusting God's character means believing his Word about who he is, regardless of how circumstances appear.

H - Hold Fast to Hope

The final question asks: Does this thought lead to biblical hope or despair? Truth always leads to hope because it connects us to God's promises and his ability to work in every situation. Even difficult truths—like conviction of sin or acknowledgment of genuine problems—lead to hope because they point toward God's solutions and grace.

Biblical hope isn't wishful thinking or denial of reality. It's confident expectation based on God's promises and past faithfulness. Thoughts that eliminate hope, declare situations hopeless, or suggest that God is finished with you contradict the fundamental message of Scripture.

Lies specialize in stealing hope by presenting temporary circumstances as permanent realities or by minimizing God's power to change situations. Truth restores hope by reminding you of God's promises, his track record of faithfulness, and his ability to work miracles in impossible situations.

Using the TRUTH framework becomes more natural with practice. Initially, you might need to consciously work through each question when evaluating thoughts. Over time, this process becomes more intuitive, allowing you to quickly identify and reject deceptive thoughts while embracing God's truth.

The framework is particularly helpful during intense emotional seasons when thoughts feel especially compelling. Emotions can make lies seem convincing, but the TRUTH framework provides objective criteria that aren't swayed by how you're feeling in the moment. It anchors your evaluation in Scripture rather than in subjective experience.

Creating Your Personal Truth Arsenal

Mental and spiritual battles require preparation, and the most effective warriors are those who have equipped themselves with the right weapons before the battle begins. Scripture calls God's Word a sword, and memorizing specific verses creates a personal arsenal of "fighting words" that can defeat lies when they arise. Creating your personal truth arsenal isn't about collecting random Bible verses—it's about strategically gathering specific truths that address your most common mental and spiritual battles.

The concept of a truth arsenal acknowledges that spiritual warfare is personal and specific. While Satan uses some universal lies against all believers, he also customizes his attacks based on your particular vulnerabilities, past experiences, and areas of struggle. This means your truth arsenal should be personalized to address the specific lies you encounter most frequently.

Begin by identifying your most common mental battles. These might include lies about your worth, fears about the future, guilt over past mistakes, doubts about God's love, anxiety about provision, or discouragement about personal growth. Most people have three to five primary areas where lies tend to gain traction. These are your spiritual weak points that require the strongest biblical reinforcement.

For each area of struggle, identify specific verses that directly address the lies you encounter. When the enemy tries to convince you that you're worthless, you can fight back with John 3:16, which declares Jesus found you worthy of his sacrifice. When fear tries to overwhelm you, respond with 2 Timothy 1:7: "For God has not given us a spirit of fear, but of power and of love and of sound mind."

Your truth arsenal should include verses about God's character, your identity in Christ, his promises for your situation, and his power to change circumstances. Don't limit yourself to "positive" verses—include truths about God's discipline, the reality of spiritual warfare, and the call to perseverance. Sometimes the most powerful truth is acknowledging that difficulty is normal and temporary.

Memorization is crucial for building an effective arsenal. You can't fight lies with truth you have to look up on your phone. When lies attack, they often arrive with emotional intensity that makes it difficult to think clearly or remember where to find relevant verses. Memorized Scripture is immediately available and doesn't require external resources.

Start with a manageable goal—perhaps memorizing one verse per week that addresses a specific area of struggle. Choose verses that resonate personally and that you can understand and apply practically. Some people find it helpful to memorize several verses that address the same lie, creating multiple weapons for particularly persistent battles.

Place verses around your home, use them as phone backgrounds, or create reminders that keep God's truth front and center. The goal is to saturate your environment with truth so that lies have less opportunity to take root. When your mental environment is filled with Scripture, there's less room for deception to grow.

Beyond individual verses, include broader biblical truths in your arsenal. Understand core doctrines like justification, sanctification, and glorification. Know the attributes of God. Understand your position in Christ and the promises available to believers. These foundational truths provide context for specific verses and help you recognize lies that contradict essential Christian doctrines.

Your truth arsenal should also include practical strategies for applying Scripture. In religious cognitive therapy, clients are taught to use their religious teachings to replace negative and inaccurate thoughts with positive principles found in Scripture that promote mental health. This might include specific prayers, declarations, or meditation practices that help you internalize and apply biblical truth.

Consider creating written resources for your arsenal. Some people find it helpful to write out their most important verses on cards they can carry with them. Others create a "truth journal" where they record verses along with personal notes about how these truths apply to their specific situations. Digital tools can also be helpful—apps that deliver verses at specific times or audio recordings of yourself reading your key verses.

Your arsenal should include verses for different types of battles. Have verses ready for when you're facing fear, discouragement, temptation, confusion, guilt, or spiritual attack. Include promises for provision, protection, guidance, and growth. Don't forget verses that address God's love, grace, forgiveness, and faithfulness—these are often the most powerful weapons against condemnation and shame.

Regular maintenance of your arsenal is important. As you grow spiritually and face new challenges, you may need to add new verses or retire others that no longer address your current battles. This doesn't mean the old verses are no longer true—it simply means your spiritual needs are evolving as you mature in faith.

Practice using your arsenal regularly, not just during intense battles. Fighting lies requires going on offense—a defensive posture is not enough. This means regularly meditating on truth, declaring it over your life, and using it to shape your thinking patterns. The more familiar you become with your arsenal during peaceful times, the more effectively you can use it during spiritual storms.

Share your arsenal with trusted friends or family members who can remind you of truth when you're struggling to remember it yourself. Speaking the truth over one another has power, and as you make a habit of affirming others, you'll find it easier to challenge your own lies. Sometimes the most powerful way to access your truth arsenal is through the voice of someone who loves you and knows God's Word.

Remember that your truth arsenal is not a magic formula that automatically eliminates all mental and spiritual struggles. It's a tool that helps you engage in spiritual warfare from a position of strength and truth. God himself is our biggest advocate in fighting Satan and his lies, and we must pray continually for a renewed mind, victory over temptation, and the ability to believe and obey God.

Building and maintaining your personal truth arsenal is a lifelong process that grows stronger and more effective over time. As you consistently use Scripture to battle lies and embrace truth, you'll find that your mind becomes increasingly aligned with God's perspective, and the lies that once held power over you lose their ability to deceive and discourage you.

CHAPTER 6: PILLAR THREE - REPLACE AND REDIRECT

You've learned to capture rogue thoughts before they capture you. You've discovered how to test every mental message against the unshakeable truth of Scripture. Now comes the third pillar of biblical thought management—perhaps the most transformative of all: learning to replace destructive thoughts with God's truth and redirect your mental energy toward what really matters. This isn't about suppressing negative thoughts or pretending problems don't exist. It's about the revolutionary practice of intentionally filling your mind with the thoughts, perspectives, and priorities of Jesus Christ himself.

Think of your mind as a garden. You can spend all your time pulling weeds, but unless you plant good seeds, the weeds will simply return stronger than before. The third pillar teaches you not just to remove mental weeds, but to cultivate a thriving garden of biblical thinking. This is where the rubber meets the road in spiritual warfare—where you move from defense to offense, from simply blocking lies to actively building truth. When you master the art of replacing and redirecting your thoughts, you're not just managing your mind; you're participating in the divine work of transformation that God designed to happen in every believer's life. The apostle Paul called this process "putting on the mind of Christ," and it's available to every Christian who's willing to engage in the beautiful, challenging work of intentional thinking.

The Power of Intentional Thinking

Most people live their entire lives as passive recipients of whatever thoughts happen to wander into their minds. They experience thoughts like they experience weather—as something that happens to them rather than something they can influence. But Scripture presents a radically different approach: the practice of intentional thinking, where you take active responsibility for directing your mental energy toward what serves God's purposes in your life.

Intentional thinking is the conscious choice to focus your mental resources on specific truths, perspectives, and goals that align with God's Word. It's the difference between drifting wherever your emotions take you and steering your thoughts toward destinations that honor Christ. This isn't about positive thinking or mental manipulation—it's about cooperating with God's design for human consciousness and allowing his truth to shape your mental landscape.

The biblical foundation for intentional thinking is found throughout Scripture, but perhaps nowhere more clearly than in Philippians 4:8: "Finally, brothers and sisters, whatever is true, whatever is noble, whatever is right, whatever is pure, whatever is lovely, whatever is admirable—if anything is excellent or praiseworthy—think about such things." Notice the active verb: "think about." Paul isn't suggesting that good thoughts will automatically fill your mind. He's commanding intentional focus on specific categories of truth.

This practice becomes especially powerful when we understand the neurological reality behind it. Modern neuroscience has discovered that thoughts alone can switch on and off genes and directly influence the cells in your body. We can turn on behavior dependent genes that drive inflammation and disease and we can turn them off. More remarkably, when you think new thoughts, you build new neural pathways, literally rewiring your brain to think differently.

This scientific reality aligns perfectly with the biblical concept of mind renewal. Romans 12:2 instructs us to "be transformed by the renewing of your mind," and we now know that such renewal involves actual structural changes in the brain. What we want to do with self-directed neuroplasticity is to consciously pursue wholesome goals, and this happens through the consistent practice of intentional thinking.

The power of intentional thinking becomes evident when you consider its opposite: passive mental wandering. When you don't intentionally direct your thoughts, your mind tends to default to familiar patterns—often negative ones. We are creatures of habit. Our thoughts produce biochemical reactions in the brain, sending signals to the body, and our bodies begin to feel in similar ways to how we were thinking. Without intention, these automatic patterns continue to dominate your mental landscape.

Intentional thinking requires understanding the difference between thoughts and attention. Thoughts are mental events that arise spontaneously, while attention is the conscious focus you bring to specific thoughts or ideas. You can't control every thought that enters your mind, but you can control where you direct your attention. When a destructive thought arises, you don't have to feed it with your attention. Instead, you can intentionally redirect your mental focus to truth.

This practice becomes transformative when you realize that your thoughts, words, and new experiences actually shape your brain. Every time you intentionally focus on God's truth instead of entertaining a lie, you're literally rewiring your neural pathways. With neuroplasticity, repetition is key. Don't be surprised when those old thoughts emerge; instead shrug them off as old neural pathways and choose to embrace the truth. Eventually, the new thoughts will take root and dominate your thinking.

The key to developing intentional thinking is starting small and building consistency. Begin with brief moments throughout your day when you consciously choose what to think about. When you wake up, instead of immediately worrying about your schedule, intentionally focus on a verse about God's faithfulness. When you're stuck in traffic, instead of fuming about delays, use the time to meditate on God's sovereignty. These small choices compound over time, creating new mental habits.

One of the most powerful aspects of intentional thinking is its proactive nature. Instead of waiting for negative thoughts to arise and then trying to combat them, you fill your mind with truth before lies have a chance to take root. Keep thinking "I'm not good/expert enough," and your brain strengthens pathways — reinforces that lie. If you constantly fear being visible online — your brain strengthens pathways of anxiety and fear. But when you consistently focus on God's truth about your identity and purpose, you strengthen different pathways entirely.

Intentional thinking also involves understanding your thought triggers—the circumstances, emotions, or experiences that tend to activate destructive mental patterns. By identifying these triggers, you can prepare specific truths to focus on when they arise. If financial stress typically triggers thoughts of scarcity and fear, you can prepare verses about God's provision. If relationship conflict usually leads to thoughts of rejection, you can focus on truths about your acceptance in Christ.

The practice requires patience with yourself as you develop this new skill. If an individual desires to transform their negative thinking into Christ-like thoughts, they may begin conscientiously studying the Word of God. The more time that is spent reading the Word of God, in prayer, and engaging in Christlike activities such as forgiveness or helping, the more efficient those Christ-grounded neural pathways become. This transformation doesn't happen overnight, but consistent practice creates lasting change.

Remember that intentional thinking isn't about denying reality or avoiding difficult emotions. It's about choosing how you interpret and respond to life's challenges. When facing genuine problems, intentional thinking helps you approach them from God's perspective rather than from fear or despair. You acknowledge the difficulty while simultaneously focusing on God's faithfulness, wisdom, and power to work in every situation.

Biblical Meditation Techniques

Biblical meditation is fundamentally different from the emptying of the mind promoted in Eastern traditions. While secular meditation often seeks to quiet thoughts entirely, Christian meditation is not an emptying of the mind. Rather, it is filling your mind with God's Word to replace negative or sinful thoughts. This practice has deep roots in Jewish and Christian tradition, predating modern mindfulness movements by thousands of years.

The Hebrew word for meditation, hagah, appears throughout the Old Testament and carries a sense of murmuring, pondering, or softly repeating—suggesting that meditation is not passive but deeply attentive. When the Psalmist declares in Psalm 1:2 that the blessed person meditates on God's law "day and night," he's describing an active, ongoing engagement with Scripture that transforms the entire orientation of one's life.

Meditation is like chewing. It is slow and thorough. Just as physical chewing breaks down food for better absorption, biblical meditation breaks down Scripture so its truths can be fully absorbed into your mind and heart. This process takes time and intentionality—it cannot be rushed or treated as a quick spiritual exercise.

One of the most foundational biblical meditation techniques is Lectio Divina, which means "divine reading." This ancient practice involves four movements: reading, meditation, prayer, and contemplation. First, you read the verse or passage of Scripture. Next, you quietly meditate on it. Third, you pray over what you just learned. Finally, you take a moment to contemplate the Scripture again, inviting the Holy Spirit to illuminate your experience.

The reading phase involves selecting a passage and reading it slowly, perhaps multiple times. Most people find it helpful to memorize the text and read it aloud several times, which was the ancient practice and is still widely used today. This isn't speed reading for information—it's careful attention to each word and phrase, allowing the text to speak to you rather than bringing your own agenda to it.

During the meditation phase, you ponder the passage deeply, asking questions like: What does this reveal about God's character? How does this apply to my current situation? What is God saying to me through these words? Write notes about what you see in this passage. Make connections between the various sections. Ask yourself, "What do these words from God say?" "What do they mean?" Place who you are and what you do next to this passage and ask God to examine you.

The prayer phase involves responding to God based on what you've discovered in the text. This might include confession, thanksgiving, requests, or simply expressing your heart to God. Pray using the passage as an outline for your prayer. Read the passage phrase-by-phrase, responding to God after each phrase or verse. This creates a dialogue between you and God through his Word.

Contemplation involves sitting quietly in God's presence, allowing what you've read and prayed to settle into your heart. Wait in stillness once more. Ask that God bring to your mind any areas of your life that you need to shape more closely to His design as revealed in this passage. Contemplate God's love and power as it is revealed here. This isn't about forcing insights but about creating space for the Holy Spirit to work.

Another powerful technique is contemplative prayer, which involves choosing a short scripture or biblical passage and reflecting on it throughout the day. This practice helps internalize the scripture and make it relevant to your life. You might select a single verse in the morning and return to it throughout the day, allowing its truth to shape your responses to various situations.

Sacred word meditation is another biblical technique where you silently repeat a sacred word, passage, or scripture with your breath. This might involve phrases like "The Lord is my shepherd," "Be still and know that I am God," or simply "Jesus." This practice anchors the mind, focusing on God's presence and can be particularly helpful during stressful or anxious moments.

Visualization meditation involves imaginatively entering biblical scenes. Some people also visualize scenes from the life of Jesus, or other biblical tales, in order to create a more engaged experience. This isn't about creating fictional scenarios but about placing yourself within the biblical narrative to understand it more personally. You might imagine walking with Jesus by the Sea of Galilee or standing with the disciples on the Mount of Transfiguration.

Breath-centered meditation on Scripture combines the physical act of breathing with biblical truth. One technique that you might consider is breath prayer, which involves taking slow, deep breaths and reciting a short prayer with each inhale and exhale. You might inhale while thinking "God is" and exhale while thinking "with me," or breathe in "I can do" and breathe out "all things through Christ."

Guided biblical meditation can be helpful for those just beginning this practice. Most guided meditation CDs start with relaxation exercises followed by a scriptural narrative. Some focus on biblical stories, while others offer visualizations like walking through nature or nailing your cares to the cross. While external guidance can be beneficial, the goal is eventually to develop your own practice of engaging directly with Scripture.

The key to effective biblical meditation is consistency rather than duration. Schedule a 15-minute quiet time every day to read the Bible, do a devotional, journal your thoughts, pray, or listen to worship music. Learn about God's true nature and begin to believe just one promise he makes in his Word. Even brief periods of meditation can be transformative when practiced regularly.

Remember that biblical meditation is both a spiritual discipline and a relational practice. You're not just studying information—you're encountering the living God through his Word. In the Christian tradition, this kind of sacred pondering becomes a bridge between the mind and the heart, between knowledge and intimacy. The goal isn't just to understand Scripture intellectually but to allow it to transform your entire being.

Rewiring Your Mental Pathways

The human brain possesses an extraordinary capacity that neuroscientists call neuroplasticity—the ability to reorganize itself by forming new neural connections throughout life. This remarkable feature means that the destructive thought patterns that may have dominated your mind for years are not permanent fixtures. Brain cells and brain networks work together in use-dependent ways, and with awareness, intention, and practice, we can strengthen those connections between neurons, leading to improved performance and well-being.

For Christians, understanding neuroplasticity provides scientific validation for what Scripture has always taught: that minds can be renewed and transformed. According to modern neuroscience, the process of reframing one's thoughts involves physiological adaptations in the brain. When Paul instructs believers to "be transformed by the renewing of your mind" in Romans 12:2, he's describing a process that involves actual changes in brain structure and function.

The mechanism behind this transformation involves what neuroscientists call "use-dependent" brain change. Every time we think a thought and generate a feeling, we install neurological hardware that impacts our well-being in all moments. When you repeatedly focus on God's truth instead of entertaining lies, you literally strengthen the neural pathways associated with biblical thinking while weakening the pathways connected to destructive thoughts.

This process requires understanding both the problem and the solution. Without intention, our feelings, thoughts, and routines automatically recycle, producing the same behaviors and choices. Your brain naturally gravitates toward familiar patterns, even if those patterns are harmful. This is why breaking free from negative thinking requires more than willpower—it requires rewiring the actual pathways in your brain.

The rewiring process begins with recognition. As you go about your day, slow down and play the curious observer of yourself to recognize when the cares of this world distract you from God or bring you back into old thought patterns. This awareness is crucial because you can't change patterns you don't recognize. When you notice destructive thoughts arising, that recognition itself begins the rewiring process.

The next step involves conscious redirection. Pause your thoughts and remember what God says instead. This isn't about suppressing negative thoughts but about choosing to focus your attention on truth. When our brains change, our minds change, because our mind is the brain in action. Each time you redirect your focus from lies to truth, you're creating new neural connections.

Repetition is absolutely essential for effective rewiring. The more time that is spent reading the Word of God, in prayer, and engaging in Christlike activities such as forgiveness or helping, the more efficient those Christ-grounded neural pathways become. Overtime, through repeated stimulation of Christ-like neural networks from engagement in Christ-like behaviors, thoughts, and experiences, the mind has the potential to effortlessly think and perform thoughts that are based on the Word of God.

This process requires patience because our brains prune away connections or synapses that we no longer use or need, while sprouting connections when we learn something new. Old thought patterns don't disappear immediately—they weaken gradually as you stop using them and strengthen new patterns instead. This is why consistency matters more than intensity in the rewiring process.

Understanding the spiritual dimension of neuroplasticity is crucial for Christians. While neuroscience explains the mechanism, it's important to recognize that spiritual growth or connection with the Holy Spirit or coming to take on the likeness of Christ has something to do in some key way with changes in their brain, but it cannot be reduced to merely physical processes. The Holy Spirit works through natural means, including neuroplasticity, to transform believers.

One of the most important aspects of rewiring involves replacing automatic thoughts with conscious choices. If you have a regular pattern that you drive everyday and you want to take a slightly different route or go to a slightly different place, if you don't think consciously about it, you'll find yourself driving to the place you always go instead of the place where you wanted to go. Similarly, without conscious intervention, your mind will default to familiar thought patterns.

The goal is to make consulting God's truth a part of your automatic response system. One of the best ways of doing that is getting oneself into the habit of consulting the Holy Spirit. Consequently, the Holy Spirit—your wise, internal advocate (to evoke the Gospel term Paraclete)—becomes a part of your habit mechanism. This creates new automatic responses based on spiritual wisdom rather than fleshly reactions.

Practical steps for rewiring include creating environmental cues that prompt biblical thinking. Place verses around your home or use them as a phone background. Keep reminders of God's truth front and center. These visual reminders help interrupt old patterns and prompt new ones. The more you expose your brain to biblical truth, the more likely you are to think biblical thoughts.

Another important aspect involves understanding what neuroscientists call "specificity." Dr. Perry states, "In order to change any part of the brain, that specific part of the brain must be activated". This means that rewiring requires engaging with the specific types of thoughts and emotions you want to change. If you struggle with anxiety, you need to practice biblical responses to anxious thoughts. If you battle with anger, you need to repeatedly choose forgiveness and grace.

The rewiring process also involves creating new experiences that support new thinking patterns. When you experience new things, your brain grows stronger connections. This might involve putting yourself in situations where you practice trusting God, serving others, or stepping out in faith. These experiences create new neural pathways that support spiritual growth.

Remember that rewiring is both a spiritual and physical process. While you're working to change your brain, you're also cooperating with God's transforming work in your life. From a biblical perspective, the changing (or retraining) of our physical brain is the result of our Spirit-directed and Spirit-generated obedience to the biblical commands, not the cause of this transformation. The physical changes support spiritual transformation, but they don't create it.

Thinking Like Jesus in Real Time

The ultimate goal of biblical thought management isn't just to eliminate negative thinking—it's to develop the actual mind of Christ. When we became Christians, we were given the Holy Spirit to live in us and with Him the mind of Christ. There is nothing more basic to the Christian life than this. But having access to Christ's mind and actually thinking with it are two different things. Learning to think like Jesus in real time requires intentional development of his perspectives, priorities, and responses.

When we have the mind of Christ we have His views, His feelings, His temperament, and we are influenced by His Spirit. This isn't about perfection but about growing alignment with how Jesus himself would think and respond in various situations. It involves developing what one theologian called "the ability to know what was in man"—the keen insight and wisdom that characterized Jesus' earthly ministry.

Thinking like Jesus begins with understanding his fundamental perspectives on life. Jesus consistently viewed situations from an eternal perspective rather than a temporary one. When facing opposition, he saw beyond immediate circumstances to God's greater purposes. When encountering suffering, he understood it within the context of redemption and glory. Jesus consistently viewed situations from an eternal perspective rather than a temporary one. This eternal mindset shapes how you interpret everything from daily frustrations to major life challenges.

Jesus also demonstrated remarkable compassion in his thinking. We will be compassionate when others are severe; we will be severe when others are tolerant; we will be kind to the ugly. His compassion wasn't sentimental but was grounded in truth and motivated by love. Learning to think like Jesus means developing his heart for people—seeing them as he sees them, with both their potential and their need for redemption.

Another characteristic of Jesus' thinking was his perfect integration of truth and grace. He never compromised truth for the sake of acceptance, nor did he wield truth as a weapon to wound people. A person with the mind of Christ should be able to discern false teachings like Doppler radar detecting a storm, while simultaneously showing patience and love toward those who are deceived.

Developing real-time thinking like Jesus requires understanding his priorities. Jesus didn't mince words about false teachers, but he also said the greatest commandments were to love God and love others. His thinking was always filtered through these priorities. When you face decisions or challenges, asking "How would this decision reflect love for God and love for people?" helps align your thinking with Christ's.

Jesus also demonstrated perfect trust in the Father's sovereignty and goodness. Even in his darkest hour, he maintained confidence in God's ultimate plan and purposes. Having the mind of Christ means realizing God cares about how we spend our time and trusting that he is working all things together for good. This trust shapes how you think about setbacks, delays, and disappointments.

One of the most challenging aspects of thinking like Jesus involves his perspective on suffering and sacrifice. Greater love has no one than this: to lay down one's life for one's friends. Jesus consistently chose the path of sacrifice when it served others and honored the Father. Learning to think like him means considering how your choices affect others and being willing to lay down your own preferences for their benefit.

Practical application of thinking like Jesus involves developing what could be called "Jesus filters" for common situations. When someone treats you unfairly, instead of immediately thinking about revenge or self-protection, you can ask: "How did Jesus respond to unfair treatment?" When facing financial pressure, instead of panicking, you can consider: "What did Jesus teach about God's provision?"

Jesus also demonstrated remarkable wisdom in knowing when to speak and when to remain silent, when to confront and when to show mercy. We need to see people with eyes of faith in Jesus's offer of salvation and the ability to change them, and then help them see Jesus with eyes of faith. This requires developing spiritual discernment that goes beyond human wisdom to understand situations from God's perspective.

Another crucial aspect of thinking like Jesus involves his perfect obedience to the Father's will. We should live to please God as Jesus did. This means filtering decisions through the question: "What would please the Father in this situation?" rather than "What would make me most comfortable or successful?"

The practical development of Christ's mind requires what Johannes Kepler called "Thinking God's thoughts after Him". This involves immersing yourself so deeply in Scripture that biblical principles become your automatic responses. Scripture is the expression of the mind of God. We understand His mind by hearing, reading, studying, and meditating on the Scripture.

Developing real-time Christ-like thinking also requires understanding that the mind of Christ is impossible without the miraculous work of the Holy Spirit. You cannot manufacture Christ's perspectives through human effort alone. This thinking develops through prayer, surrender, and dependence on the Spirit's guidance. It's a supernatural transformation that happens as you yield your mind to God's influence.

The goal isn't perfection but progress. Unless we grasp this we will not make any significant or lasting change or progress in our

Christian life. Significant or lasting change in beliefs or behaviour depends on a change of mind first. Every time you choose to think like Jesus instead of thinking like the world, you're participating in the ongoing transformation that God desires for every believer.

Remember that thinking like Jesus doesn't mean thinking exactly as he thought—you're not trying to become Jesus. Rather, you're learning to think with his values, his priorities, his love, and his wisdom. Cultivating a mind like Christ is important; in order to flourish in the life that God gave us, we must "take every thought captive to obey Christ". This is the daily practice of allowing his perspectives to shape your responses to every situation you encounter.

CHAPTER 7: DEFEATING THE WORRY MONSTER

There's a monster living in millions of minds today, and it feeds on uncertainty, grows stronger with each "what if," and thrives in the darkness of endless overthinking. This monster has many names—anxiety, worry, fear, panic—but its goal is always the same: to convince you that danger lurks around every corner and that peace is an impossible dream. If you've ever felt your heart race over situations beyond your control, if you've lost sleep to spinning thoughts, or if you've found yourself paralyzed by fears that seem larger than life, you've encountered this creature firsthand.

But here's what the worry monster doesn't want you to know: it's not as powerful as it pretends to be. Despite its loud roar and intimidating presence, this monster operates on deception, feeding you lies about your future, your safety, and God's faithfulness. The truth is, you don't have to live under its tyranny. God has equipped you with everything you need not just to survive the attacks of anxiety, but to defeat them entirely. Through understanding how your brain works, applying biblical wisdom, and implementing practical strategies rooted in faith, you can starve this monster of its power and reclaim the peace that is your birthright as a child of God. This chapter will arm you with the knowledge and tools you need to send the worry monster packing—not just temporarily, but permanently.

Understanding Anxiety's Grip on Your Mind

Anxiety operates like a sophisticated security system gone haywire. What was originally designed to protect you from genuine danger has become hypersensitive, triggering false alarms at the slightest provocation. To defeat anxiety, you must first understand how it works—its mechanisms, its triggers, and why it feels so overwhelming when it strikes. Knowledge is power, and understanding anxiety's grip on your mind is the first step toward loosening its hold.

At its core, anxiety is your brain's response to perceived threat. When your brain detects something it interprets as dangerous, it initiates a complex cascade of neurological and physiological changes designed to help you survive. This process begins in a small, almond-shaped region called the amygdala, often referred to as your brain's "alarm system." The amygdala's job is to scan your environment for threats and sound the alarm when danger is detected.

The amygdala doesn't distinguish between real and imagined threats. Whether you're facing a genuine physical danger or simply thinking about a challenging conversation with your boss next week, your amygdala can trigger the same intense response. This is why anxiety can feel so physically overwhelming—your body is preparing for a life-or-death situation even when you're sitting safely in your living room worrying about tomorrow's presentation.

When the amygdala sounds its alarm, it sends signals to the hypothalamus, which activates your sympathetic nervous system. This triggers the release of stress hormones like adrenaline and cortisol, preparing your body for what scientists call the "fight-or-flight" response. Within milliseconds, your heart rate increases, your breathing becomes shallow, your muscles tense, and blood flows

100

away from non-essential functions toward your major muscle groups. Your pupils dilate, your hearing becomes more acute, and your brain becomes laser-focused on potential threats.

This response system worked perfectly for our ancestors who faced genuine physical dangers like predators or natural disasters. The problem is that modern anxiety rarely involves the kind of immediate physical threats this system was designed to handle. Instead, we face psychological threats—deadlines, relationship conflicts, financial pressures, health concerns—that can't be resolved by fighting or fleeing. This creates a situation where your body is revved up for intense physical action, but there's nowhere for that energy to go.

The experience becomes even more complicated when you understand how anxiety affects your prefrontal cortex—the part of your brain responsible for rational thinking, decision-making, and perspective. When anxiety strikes, blood flow shifts away from this region toward more primitive survival areas. This is why it becomes so difficult to think clearly when you're anxious. Your brain literally has reduced access to its higher-level thinking functions, making everything seem more threatening and solutions feel impossible to find.

Anxiety also hijacks your attention in ways that can make the experience feel inescapable. When you're anxious, your brain becomes hypervigilant, constantly scanning for potential threats. This creates what psychologists call "attentional bias"—you become much more likely to notice and focus on anything that could confirm your fears while filtering out information that might provide reassurance. If you're worried about your health, you'll notice every ache and pain while dismissing signs that you're actually fine. If you're anxious about a relationship, you'll fixate on any sign of distance while overlooking expressions of love and commitment.

This selective attention creates a feedback loop that strengthens anxiety over time. The more you focus on potential threats, the more threatening your world appears, which triggers more anxiety, which makes you focus even more on dangers. Before long, you can feel trapped in a cycle where anxiety seems to be everywhere and escape feels impossible.

Understanding the role of worry in this process is crucial. Worry is anxiety's favorite tool because it masquerades as problem-solving. When you worry, it feels like you're doing something productive about your concerns. In reality, worry is mental wheel-spinning that creates the illusion of progress while actually making problems feel bigger and solutions feel more elusive. Worry takes potential future problems and treats them as if they're happening right now, flooding your system with stress hormones for situations that may never occur.

The physical symptoms of anxiety can be particularly confusing and frightening. Many people experiencing anxiety for the first time genuinely believe they're having a heart attack, going crazy, or developing a serious medical condition. These symptoms—racing heart, difficulty breathing, sweating, trembling, nausea, dizziness—are actually your body's normal response to the stress hormones flooding your system. Understanding this doesn't make the symptoms less real or less uncomfortable, but it can remove the additional layer of fear that comes from not knowing what's happening to you.

Chronic anxiety creates additional complications by keeping your stress response system in a constantly activated state. When cortisol and other stress hormones remain elevated for extended periods, they begin to affect virtually every system in your body. Research suggests that chronic stress contributes to high blood pressure, promotes the formation of artery-clogging deposits, and causes brain changes that may contribute to anxiety, depression, and addiction. This is why anxiety isn't just a mental health issue—it's a whole-person problem that affects your physical health, relationships, and spiritual well-being.

For Christians, anxiety often carries an additional burden of shame. Many believers struggle with the feeling that anxiety represents a failure of faith or trust in God. This shame can actually make anxiety worse by adding self-condemnation to an already difficult experience. The truth is that anxiety doesn't discriminate based on spiritual maturity. Many of the heroes of faith in Scripture—including Moses, David, Elijah, and even Jesus himself—experienced anxiety and distress. Anxiety doesn't disqualify you from God's love, nor does it mean you're failing as a Christian.

The worry monster becomes particularly cunning when it uses partially true information to support its lies. Anxiety often takes legitimate concerns—things that genuinely need attention or prayer—and inflates them beyond all proportion. A reasonable concern about your child's safety becomes paralyzing fear that prevents you from letting them grow and experience age-appropriate independence. A legitimate financial concern becomes catastrophic thinking that assumes the worst-case scenario is inevitable.

Breaking free from anxiety's grip requires understanding that feelings are not facts. When anxiety strikes, it brings a flood of emotions and physical sensations that feel incredibly real and urgent. But the intensity of these feelings doesn't correlate with the accuracy of the thoughts that triggered them. Learning to observe your anxious thoughts and feelings without automatically believing they represent truth is a crucial skill in defeating the worry monster.

The good news is that the same neuroplasticity that allows anxiety patterns to develop also makes it possible to rewire your brain for peace. Every time you choose to respond to anxiety with faith instead of fear, every time you redirect worried thoughts to God's promises, and every time you take practical steps to care for your mental and physical health, you're literally changing your brain's structure and function. Recovery from anxiety isn't just possible—it's the normal result when you apply biblical principles and practical strategies consistently over time.

The Neuroscience of Fear and Faith

The relationship between neuroscience and faith reveals one of the most fascinating aspects of how God designed the human brain. Far from being incompatible, recent research shows that faith-based practices actually create measurable, positive changes in brain structure and function that directly counteract the effects of anxiety and fear. Understanding this neuroscientific foundation of faith provides powerful insight into why biblical approaches to anxiety are so effective.

When neuroscientists study the brains of people engaged in prayer, meditation, or other spiritual practices, they discover remarkable patterns of brain activity that promote mental health and emotional stability. Research conducted by Dr. Andrew Newberg and others in the field of neurotheology has shown that people who spend regular time in prayer or meditation demonstrate increased activity in the frontal lobes—the areas responsible for focus, attention, executive function, and emotional regulation. These are precisely the brain regions that become compromised during anxiety attacks.

The frontal lobes play a crucial role in what neuroscientists call "top-down regulation"—the brain's ability to consciously override automatic emotional responses. When these areas are strengthened through spiritual practices, you develop greater capacity to interrupt anxious thoughts before they spiral into panic. This neurological strengthening provides a biological foundation for what Scripture describes as taking thoughts captive and bringing them into obedience to Christ.

Equally significant is what happens in the parietal lobes during deep spiritual experiences. Brain imaging studies show dramatically decreased activity in the areas responsible for maintaining your sense of physical boundaries and temporal orientation. This neurological shift corresponds to the biblical experience of losing yourself in God's presence, feeling "at one" with divine love, and experiencing peace that transcends understanding. Rather than being merely subjective experiences, these spiritual states produce measurable changes in brain function.

The research on prayer is particularly relevant for understanding how faith combats anxiety. Studies have found that prayer activates brain regions associated with emotional regulation while decreasing activity in areas linked to stress and fear. When people pray—especially intercessory prayer for others—brain scans show increased activity in regions associated with compassion and decreased activity in the amygdala, the brain's fear center. This neurological pattern suggests that prayer literally rewires the brain for peace rather than panic.

One of the most significant discoveries in this field involves the relationship between faith practices and the default mode network (DMN)—a collection of brain regions that become active when your mind is at rest. In anxious individuals, the DMN often becomes hyperactive and focused on rumination and worry. However, people who regularly engage in contemplative prayer or meditation show more balanced DMN activity, with less tendency toward repetitive, anxious thinking patterns.

The neuroscience of gratitude provides another powerful example of how faith-based practices reshape the brain. When you actively practice thanksgiving—as Scripture repeatedly commands—you stimulate the release of dopamine and serotonin, neurotransmitters associated with happiness and well-being. Regular gratitude practice actually strengthens neural pathways associated with positive emotions while weakening connections linked to anxiety and depression. This explains why Paul's instruction to pray "with thanksgiving" isn't just spiritual advice—it's brain-based therapy.

Meditation on Scripture creates particularly powerful neurological changes because it combines multiple brain-healthy activities: focused attention, positive emotional content, repetitive practice, and meaning-making. When you meditate on God's Word, you're engaging multiple brain networks simultaneously in ways that promote integration and emotional regulation. Brain imaging shows that people who regularly meditate on spiritual texts develop increased gray matter density in areas associated with emotional regulation and decreased reactivity in fear-processing regions.

The concept of neuroplasticity—the brain's ability to reorganize and form new neural connections throughout life—provides hope for anyone struggling with anxiety. Every time you choose to respond to fearful thoughts with faith-based truths, you're literally rewiring your brain. Neural pathways that get used repeatedly become stronger and more automatic, while those that go unused gradually weaken. This means that consistently practicing faith-based responses to anxiety doesn't just provide temporary relief—it creates lasting changes in how your brain processes stress and threat.

The neuroscience of worship reveals additional mechanisms by which faith impacts brain function. When people engage in singing, especially in community worship settings, their brains release endorphins and oxytocin—chemicals associated with bonding, stress reduction, and emotional well-being. The rhythmic nature of many worship songs also activates the parasympathetic nervous system, which counteracts the stress response and promotes

107

relaxation. This biological basis helps explain why David could write about finding comfort in God's presence and why Scripture repeatedly encourages believers to sing praises even in difficult circumstances.

Research on religious communities shows that social connection—a key component of faith life—provides additional neurological benefits. When you fellowship with other believers, participate in communal worship, or receive prayer and support from your faith community, your brain releases oxytocin and other bonding hormones that reduce stress and promote emotional resilience. This social dimension of faith creates a buffer against anxiety that extends far beyond individual spiritual practices.

The neuroscience of hope reveals why biblical encouragement about the future has such powerful effects on present anxiety. When you focus on God's promises and maintain hope despite difficult circumstances, you activate brain regions associated with motivation and reward while dampening activity in areas linked to despair and helplessness. Hope literally changes your brain's response to current challenges by maintaining neural pathways associated with possibility and solution-finding.

Understanding the neurological basis of faith doesn't diminish its spiritual significance—rather, it reveals the incredible wisdom of God in designing brains that respond so positively to relationship with him. The same God who created your brain also provided practices and truths that promote optimal brain function. This integration of spiritual truth and neurological health demonstrates God's holistic care for your entire being.

The implications of this research are profound for anxiety management. It means that biblical practices aren't just spiritually beneficial—they're neurologically therapeutic. When you pray, meditate on Scripture, practice gratitude, worship, and maintain hope in God's promises, you're engaging in scientifically validated interventions that literally rewire your brain for peace. This doesn't minimize the need for God's supernatural intervention, but it shows how God often works through the natural processes he designed.

For those struggling with severe anxiety, this research provides hope that change is possible. Even brains that have been dominated by anxiety patterns for years can be rewired through consistent practice of faith-based interventions. The neuroplasticity research shows that it's never too late to develop new neural pathways associated with peace, and the spiritual practices that promote these changes are freely available to every believer.

The neuroscience of fear and faith ultimately reveals that God designed your brain not just to survive, but to thrive in relationship with him. Every aspect of brain function—from attention and emotion regulation to social bonding and hope—works optimally when aligned with biblical principles. This scientific validation of faith practices provides additional confidence for choosing God's ways over the world's approaches to anxiety management.

Practical Strategies for Worry-Free Living

Living free from worry isn't about pretending problems don't exist or maintaining constant positivity. It's about developing a comprehensive toolkit of biblical and practical strategies that help you navigate life's challenges with faith, wisdom, and peace. These strategies work together to address anxiety at multiple levels—spiritual, mental, physical, and relational—creating a holistic approach to worry-free living.

The foundation of worry-free living is implementing what Scripture calls "the answer to anxiety" found in Philippians 4:6-7. This passage provides a clear, actionable strategy: "Do not be anxious about anything, but in every situation, by prayer and petition, with thanksgiving, present your requests to God. And the peace of God, which transcends all understanding, will guard your hearts and your minds in Christ Jesus." This isn't just spiritual advice—it's a practical protocol for interrupting anxiety cycles.

The STOP method provides a memorable way to apply this biblical principle in real-time. When anxiety begins to rise, immediately STOP and implement these four steps: Seek God in prayer about everything; Trust God through prayers of thanksgiving; Open your mind to what comes from God; Practice the Word of God. This method interrupts anxiety's momentum and redirects your focus toward God's truth and peace.

Prayer becomes most effective for anxiety when it's specific, persistent, and saturated with thanksgiving. Instead of vague prayers like "Help me not worry," present specific requests to God with detailed thanksgiving for his past faithfulness. For example: "Father, I'm anxious about tomorrow's medical test. I thank you that you've walked with me through every health challenge in the past. I ask for your peace today and wisdom for my doctors tomorrow. I'm grateful that you know the results already and nothing surprises you."

Developing a personal Scripture arsenal specifically for anxiety creates powerful ammunition against worry. Identify 10-15 verses that directly address your most common fears and anxieties. Memorize these verses and practice bringing them to mind immediately when anxious thoughts arise. Verses like Psalm 55:22 ("Cast your cares on the Lord and he will sustain you"), Isaiah 26:3 ("You will keep in perfect peace those whose minds are steadfast, because they trust in you"), and Matthew 6:26 ("Look at the birds of the air; they do not sow or reap or store away in barns, and yet your heavenly Father feeds them. Are you not much more valuable than they?") become mental weapons against the lies of anxiety.

The practice of thought replacement is crucial because simply trying to stop anxious thoughts rarely works. When worry begins, immediately redirect your attention to one of three categories: True thoughts (based on God's Word), Reasonable thoughts (based on evidence rather than emotion), and Useful thoughts (that actually help solve problems rather than create more). This TRU method helps you distinguish between productive concern and destructive worry.

Implementing structured worry time can paradoxically reduce overall anxiety. Designate 15-20 minutes each day as your "worry appointment." When anxious thoughts arise during the day, tell yourself, "I'll think about that during my worry time," and redirect your attention to the present moment. During your designated worry time, examine your concerns rationally, develop specific action plans for things you can control, and pray about things you cannot control. This technique prevents worry from infiltrating your entire day while ensuring legitimate concerns receive appropriate attention.

Physical strategies are essential because anxiety manifests in your body as much as your mind. Regular exercise acts as a natural anxiety reliever by burning off stress hormones, releasing mood-boosting endorphins, and improving your brain's ability to regulate emotions. Even a 10-minute walk can interrupt anxiety cycles and provide immediate relief. Deep breathing exercises activate your parasympathetic nervous system, counteracting anxiety's physical symptoms. Practice the 4-7-8 technique: inhale for 4 counts, hold for 7 counts, exhale for 8 counts, and repeat 4 times.

Sleep hygiene becomes critical for anxiety management because exhaustion makes everything feel more threatening. Establish a consistent sleep schedule, create a calming bedtime routine, and avoid screens for at least an hour before bed. If racing thoughts keep you awake, keep a journal by your bed to write down concerns and commitments to address them tomorrow. This mental "parking lot" helps quiet your mind for rest.

Nutrition directly impacts anxiety levels through its effects on blood sugar, neurotransmitter production, and inflammation. Reduce caffeine intake, as it can mimic and amplify anxiety symptoms. Avoid alcohol, which provides temporary relief but ultimately increases anxiety as it metabolizes. Focus on stable blood sugar through regular, balanced meals containing protein, healthy fats, and complex carbohydrates. Consider adding omega-3 fatty acids, magnesium, and vitamin D supplements after consulting with a healthcare provider.

Cognitive strategies help you examine and challenge anxious thoughts rather than automatically accepting them as truth. When anxiety strikes, ask yourself: Is this thought true? Is this thought helpful? Is this thought kind to myself? This III method helps you evaluate whether thoughts deserve your attention and mental energy. Often, anxious thoughts fail all three tests, revealing them as mental noise rather than valuable information.

The practice of "worst-case scenario" planning can actually reduce anxiety by removing uncertainty—worry's favorite breeding ground. For legitimate concerns, deliberately think through the worst realistic outcome and develop specific plans for how you would handle it. Often, you'll discover that even worst-case scenarios are more manageable than your anxiety suggested, and having a plan reduces the feeling of helplessness that fuels worry.

Building supportive relationships provides crucial protection against anxiety because isolation amplifies worry while community provides perspective and support. Identify trusted friends or family members who can pray with you, provide practical help during stressful times, and offer wise counsel when you're struggling to see clearly. Don't hesitate to reach out for professional counseling when anxiety significantly impacts your daily functioning.

Creating environmental supports helps reinforce anxiety management strategies. Place encouraging Scripture verses where you'll see them regularly—bathroom mirrors, car dashboard, phone wallpaper, work computer. Develop calming rituals for stressful times, such as drinking herbal tea while reading Psalms or taking a hot bath while listening to worship music. These environmental cues help trigger relaxation responses and redirect your mind toward peace.

113

Time management strategies reduce anxiety by preventing the overwhelm that comes from poor planning and unrealistic expectations. Use calendars and to-do lists to manage commitments realistically. Practice saying "no" to requests that would overextend you. Build buffer time into your schedule to prevent the rush that triggers anxiety. Remember that margin isn't luxury—it's necessary for mental health.

The practice of gratitude serves as a powerful anxiety antidote because grateful and anxious thoughts cannot coexist in your mind simultaneously. Develop a daily gratitude practice, writing down three specific things you're thankful for each day. During anxious moments, immediately list five things you're grateful for in the present moment. This practice literally rewires your brain to notice blessings rather than threats.

Developing a crisis plan prepares you for times when anxiety feels overwhelming. Identify warning signs that your anxiety is escalating, specific people you can call for support, practical steps you'll take (deep breathing, prayer, taking a walk), and circumstances that would prompt you to seek professional help. Having a clear plan removes decision-making pressure during crisis moments and ensures you have access to necessary support.

Building Unshakeable Peace

True peace—the kind that remains steady during storms and grows stronger under pressure—isn't built overnight or achieved through a single strategy. It's constructed layer by layer, through consistent choices that align your heart, mind, and actions with God's truth.

Building unshakeable peace requires understanding that peace isn't the absence of problems but the presence of God's power working within you regardless of circumstances.

The foundation of unshakeable peace is what Jesus called "peace I give you" in John 14:27—a peace that operates independently of external conditions. This divine peace differs fundamentally from worldly peace, which depends on favorable circumstances, controllable outcomes, and the absence of conflict. God's peace transcends understanding precisely because it doesn't make logical sense from a human perspective. It's possible to experience profound peace while facing serious illness, financial hardship, relationship struggles, or other significant challenges.

Understanding the difference between human peace and divine peace is crucial for building lasting tranquility. Human peace is conditional, temporary, and circumstance-dependent. It requires everything to go according to plan and dissolves the moment problems arise. Divine peace, however, is unconditional, permanent, and circumstance-independent. It flows from your relationship with God rather than your relationship with circumstances, making it available even in the midst of trials.

The practice of Sabbath rest forms one of the most important pillars of unshakeable peace. God didn't design Sabbath as a suggestion for those who have time—he established it as a commandment because regular rest is essential for human flourishing. If you struggle with anxiety, you probably violate Sabbath principles by maintaining constant productivity, endless availability, and relentless busyness. Sabbath forces you to practice trust by deliberately stepping away from work and acknowledging that God manages the universe quite well without your constant involvement.

Building Sabbath rhythms starts small and grows gradually. Begin with a few hours each week dedicated entirely to rest, reflection, and renewal. Turn off devices, avoid work-related conversations, and engage in activities that restore your soul rather than deplete your energy. This might include nature walks, reading Scripture, spending unhurried time with loved ones, or pursuing hobbies that bring joy rather than stress. As you experience the peace that comes from regular rest, gradually expand these rhythms into fuller Sabbath observance.

Developing spiritual disciplines creates additional pillars supporting unshakeable peace. These aren't legalistic requirements but life-giving practices that strengthen your connection to God and build resilience against anxiety. Daily Scripture reading fills your mind with truth that counteracts worry's lies. Regular prayer maintains ongoing conversation with God rather than crisis-only communication. Worship—both corporate and personal—shifts your focus from problems to God's character and power.

The discipline of meditation on God's Word differs significantly from secular mindfulness practices, though both offer mental health benefits. Biblical meditation involves focused reflection on specific truths about God's character, promises, and ways. Choose a verse or short passage and spend extended time considering its meaning, implications, and applications to your life. This practice literally rewires your brain's default thoughts from anxiety to faith.

Fasting represents another powerful discipline for building peace, though it's often misunderstood or overlooked in contemporary Christian practice. Fasting from food for brief periods helps you recognize your dependence on God while strengthening your ability to delay gratification and resist impulses. You can also fast from other things that contribute to anxiety—social media, news consumption, shopping, or other activities that agitate rather than calm your spirit.

Creating a personal rule of life provides structure that supports peace-building practices. A rule of life isn't a rigid schedule but a flexible framework organizing your time around what matters most. Include daily practices (prayer, Scripture reading, gratitude), weekly practices (Sabbath, corporate worship, service), and seasonal practices (retreats, extended periods of prayer, life evaluation). This structure prevents important practices from being crowded out by urgent but less important activities.

The practice of surrender forms another essential pillar of unshakeable peace. Surrender isn't passive resignation but active trust that releases outcomes to God while remaining faithful in your responsibilities. This involves regularly identifying areas where you're trying to control things beyond your influence and consciously choosing to entrust them to God's care. Surrender often requires multiple repetitions for the same issue as anxiety attempts to regain control.

Building proper boundaries protects peace by preventing overcommitment, inappropriate responsibility for others' choices, and depletion of emotional resources. Biblical boundaries aren't selfish but necessary for sustainable service and healthy relationships. Learn to distinguish between your responsibilities and others' responsibilities, practice saying "no" to requests that exceed your capacity, and communicate your limits clearly and kindly.

Developing perspective habits helps maintain peace during temporary difficulties by connecting current challenges to larger spiritual realities. Practice viewing problems through eternal lenses rather than temporal ones. Ask questions like: "How might God use this situation for my growth?" "What might this teach me about dependence on him?" "How could this experience equip me to help others facing similar challenges?" This perspective doesn't minimize real difficulties but places them within the context of God's sovereign purposes.

The cultivation of hope serves as another crucial element in building unshakeable peace. Biblical hope isn't wishful thinking but confident expectation based on God's character and promises. Regularly remind yourself of God's faithfulness in past difficulties, study his promises regarding the future, and maintain focus on eternal realities that transcend temporary troubles. Hope anchors your soul when circumstances threaten to overwhelm your peace.

Community relationships provide essential support for maintaining peace during challenging seasons. Surround yourself with people who encourage faith rather than fuel anxiety, who speak truth rather than amplify worries, and who pray for you during difficult times. Be willing to ask for help when needed and equally willing to provide support for others facing their own struggles. Isolation breeds anxiety while healthy community fosters peace.

Financial stewardship contributes significantly to peace by removing money worries and demonstrating trust in God's provision. Live within your means, maintain emergency savings when possible, give generously to God's work, and avoid debt that creates ongoing anxiety. Financial peace isn't about having unlimited resources but about trusting God's provision while managing responsibly what he entrusts to your care.

The practice of contentment represents one of the highest levels of peace-building. Contentment isn't settling for less than God's best but finding satisfaction in God himself regardless of circumstances. This involves gratitude for present blessings, trust in God's timing for changes, and freedom from comparison with others' situations. Contentment must be learned through practice and doesn't come naturally in a culture that promotes constant wanting.

Finally, maintaining eternal perspective provides the ultimate foundation for unshakeable peace. Remember that this life, with all its troubles and anxieties, is temporary preparation for eternal joy in God's presence. Current difficulties, no matter how severe, are "light and momentary troubles" compared to "eternal weight of glory" (2 Corinthians 4:17). This perspective doesn't minimize present pain but provides hope that transcends temporary circumstances and builds peace that truly cannot be shaken.

CHAPTER 8: BREAKING FREE FROM GUILT AND SHAME

Guilt and shame are perhaps the most devastating weapons in the enemy's arsenal against your mind and heart. They whisper lies about your worth, replay your worst moments on endless repeat, and convince you that you're beyond the reach of God's love and grace. While guilt points an accusing finger at what you've done, shame delivers an even more crushing verdict: it declares who you are fundamentally flawed, unredeemable, and unworthy of love. These toxic emotions don't just steal your peace—they rob you of your very identity as a beloved child of God.

But here's the revolutionary truth that can shatter every chain of guilt and shame: God doesn't see you the way you see yourself when you're trapped in condemnation. He sees you through the lens of Christ's perfect sacrifice, clothed in righteousness, spotless and blameless in his sight. The same God who spoke the universe into existence has spoken a new identity over your life, and his Word carries infinitely more weight than your feelings, your past mistakes, or the condemning voices that echo in your mind. This chapter will equip you to distinguish between the conviction that leads to life and the condemnation that leads to death, to receive the healing that God offers for your deepest wounds, and to walk confidently in the freedom that Christ purchased for you at the cross. Your past does not define you—God's love does.

The Difference Between Conviction and Condemnation

Understanding the distinction between conviction and condemnation is absolutely crucial for anyone seeking freedom from guilt and shame. These two experiences may feel similar in the moment, but they originate from completely different sources, lead to entirely different destinations, and require opposite responses. Failing to distinguish between them can leave you trapped in cycles of self-condemnation when God is actually calling you toward freedom and growth.

Conviction is the Holy Spirit's loving correction designed to restore you to fellowship with God and alignment with his will. When conviction comes, it feels like a gentle but firm hand on your shoulder, pointing out specific areas where you've strayed from God's best. Conviction is precise, constructive, and always accompanied by hope. It says, "You did something wrong, but there's a path back to righteousness." The Holy Spirit convicts to lead you to repentance, not to destroy you. This is why conviction, though initially uncomfortable, ultimately produces peace, freedom, and spiritual growth.

Condemnation, by contrast, comes from the enemy and represents his attempt to keep you trapped in shame and separation from God. Condemnation speaks in absolutes, declaring you fundamentally flawed rather than addressing specific behaviors. It says, "You are bad," rather than "You did something bad." Where conviction offers hope and a way forward, condemnation offers only despair and death. Romans 8:1 makes this crystal clear: "There is therefore now no condemnation for those who are in Christ Jesus." If you're experiencing condemnation, it's not coming from God.

The difference in tone between conviction and condemnation is striking. Conviction whispers, "You are way too magnificent and pure to be acting like that. Don't act less than who I say you are!" It appeals to your true identity in Christ and calls you to live up to who God says you are. Condemnation, however, screams accusations, brings up past failures that have already been forgiven, and seeks to convince you that you're beyond redemption. Condemnation wants to bring up the past and dwell on stuff God cast into the deepest ocean.

The source of these messages reveals their true nature. Conviction comes from the Holy Spirit, who Jesus called the Paraclete—your wise, internal advocate. The Spirit convicts because he loves you and wants to protect you from the consequences of sin while drawing you closer to God. Condemnation comes from Satan, whom Scripture calls "the accuser of the brethren." His goal is not correction but destruction, not restoration but separation from God.

The timing of these messages also differs significantly. Conviction typically comes before or during sinful behavior, serving as a warning or immediate correction. It's the gentle voice that says, "Don't go down that path" or "Stop and choose differently." Condemnation often comes after the fact, bringing up failures that have already been confessed and forgiven. If you've already repented of something and given it to Jesus, then trust you are forgiven! Condemnation wants to make you relive and rehearse forgiven failures.

The emotional trajectory of conviction versus condemnation reveals their distinct purposes. When you respond appropriately to conviction—through confession, repentance, and receiving God's forgiveness—you experience relief, freedom, joy, and increased intimacy with God. Your relationship with him is restored, and you feel cleaner and closer to him than before. Condemnation, however, produces an entirely different emotional outcome: shame, despair, hopelessness, and the desire to hide from God rather than run to him.

Physical manifestations often accompany these spiritual experiences. Conviction may initially produce a healthy sense of sorrow over sin—what Scripture calls "godly sorrow"—but this quickly transforms into peace and joy once you've responded appropriately. Condemnation, however, produces what the Bible calls "worldly sorrow" that leads to death. This includes feelings of heaviness, depression, panic, and the physical symptoms of shame such as the desire to hide, isolate, or engage in destructive behaviors.

The scope of the message helps distinguish conviction from condemnation. Conviction addresses specific behaviors, attitudes, or choices that need correction. It provides clear direction about what needs to change and how to change it. Condemnation attacks your entire identity, using vague accusations that are difficult to address because they target who you are rather than what you've done. Conviction says, "That behavior doesn't reflect who you are in Christ." Condemnation says, "You're a terrible person."

The duration of these experiences also differs. Conviction leads to quick resolution through confession and repentance. Once you've acknowledged your sin and received God's forgiveness, conviction accomplishes its purpose and lifts. Condemnation, however, is persistent and relentless. It doesn't ease when you confess because it's not coming from God and therefore doesn't respond to spiritual solutions. Instead, it must be recognized as a lie and rejected.

Your response to these experiences reveals their true nature. Conviction draws you toward God, prompting prayer, confession, and a desire for righteousness. It makes you want to get right with God and others you may have wronged. Condemnation drives you away from God, making you feel like you're too dirty, too shameful, or too far gone to approach him. It produces the Adam and Eve response—hiding from God rather than running to him.

The fruit of these experiences provides perhaps the clearest distinction. Conviction produces repentance that leads to salvation and leaves no regret, as Paul writes in 2 Corinthians 7:10. It results in spiritual growth, stronger relationships, and increased freedom. Condemnation produces what Paul calls "worldly sorrow" that brings death. It leads to spiritual stagnation, broken relationships, and increasing bondage.

Understanding these differences empowers you to respond appropriately to each experience. When you recognize conviction, respond with humility, confession, and gratitude for God's loving correction. When you recognize condemnation, reject it immediately and remind yourself of your identity in Christ. Don't engage with condemnation by trying to defend yourself or analyze whether it's true—simply recognize it as an enemy attack and declare the truth about who you are in Christ.

The practical application of this knowledge can transform your spiritual life. Instead of accepting every guilty feeling as legitimate, you can evaluate the source, tone, and fruit of these experiences. This discernment protects you from false guilt while ensuring you remain sensitive to the Holy Spirit's genuine conviction. It prevents the enemy from using fake guilt to manipulate you while preserving your ability to grow through God's loving correction.

Healing from Past Mistakes

One of the greatest barriers to emotional and spiritual freedom is the inability to release ourselves from the prison of past mistakes. Many Christians live in a constant state of regret, replaying failures and believing lies about their worth based on their worst moments. This chronic self-condemnation not only steals present joy but also hinders future growth by keeping you focused on what you've done wrong rather than what God is doing right in your life.

The first step in healing from past mistakes is understanding God's perspective on your failures. When God forgives, Scripture tells us that he remembers our sin no more. This doesn't mean God develops divine amnesia—it means he chooses not to hold your sins against you or bring up your sin in a negative way. Psalm 103:12 declares that "as far as the east is from the west, so far has he removed our transgressions from us." Notice that east and west never meet—they represent infinite distance, indicating that God has placed infinite distance between you and your forgiven sins.

The reason many Christians struggle to move beyond past mistakes is that they're trying to be more righteous than God himself. If God has chosen to forgive and forget, who are you to continue condemning yourself? When God forgives each one of us, he promises to remember our sin no more. God in all his infinite power and wisdom chooses not to hold your sins against you. If God promises to never remind you of your sin, why won't you forgive yourself for your past mistakes?

Self-forgiveness isn't selfish—it's actually a biblical mandate. Jesus commanded us to "love your neighbor as yourself" (Matthew 22:39). This implies that you should treat others with the same love, mercy, and forgiveness you extend to yourself. When you harbor negative feelings and emotions toward yourself, you're likely to do the same toward others. You cannot properly love and forgive others until you first have learned to forgive yourself.

The process of healing from past mistakes requires both receiving God's forgiveness and extending forgiveness to yourself. This involves several practical steps. First, honestly acknowledge what you've done wrong without minimizing or making excuses. Take full responsibility for your actions and their consequences. This isn't about wallowing in guilt but about taking ownership so you can move forward in truth.

Second, confess your sins to God, trusting in his promise that "if we confess our sins, he is faithful and just to forgive us our sins and to cleanse us from all unrighteousness" (1 John 1:9). Notice that God not only forgives but also cleanses. He removes the offense completely and cleanses you from ALL unrighteousness. When God cleans something, he doesn't leave a spot. It's perfect.

Third, make amends where possible and appropriate. This might involve apologizing to people you've hurt, restoring what you've damaged, or making changes to prevent similar failures in the future. The goal isn't to earn forgiveness—God's forgiveness is already freely given—but to demonstrate repentance and restore relationships where possible.

Fourth, build tolerance for remorse without allowing it to define your worth. Remorse is a natural and healthy response to wrongdoing, but it becomes destructive when it transforms into identity-defining shame. Learn to feel remorse without allowing it to convince you that you're a bad person. You can acknowledge "I did something wrong" without accepting "I am something wrong."

Fifth, expand your awareness of larger truths about yourself and your situation. Forgiveness requires seeing the bigger picture, including your own layers of brokenness, the circumstances that contributed to your failures, and God's redemptive purposes in allowing difficult experiences. This doesn't excuse wrongdoing but provides context that can help diffuse the intensity of self-condemnation.

The healing process often involves confronting lies you've believed about yourself based on past mistakes. Common lies include: "I'm beyond redemption," "God could never forgive someone like me," "I've ruined my life permanently," "I'll always struggle with this," and "I'm not like other Christians who have it together." Each of these lies must be identified and replaced with biblical truth about God's character, his forgiveness, and your identity in Christ.

Sometimes healing from past mistakes requires addressing deeper issues such as perfectionism, people-pleasing, or fear of rejection that contributed to the original failures. These underlying issues often drive behavior patterns that lead to repeated mistakes. Healing involves not just addressing the symptoms (the mistakes) but also treating the root causes (the heart issues) that produced them.

The concept of restitution plays an important role in healing from some past mistakes. While God's forgiveness is complete and unconditional, there may still be practical consequences that need to be addressed. If you've stolen, you may need to return what you took. If you've damaged relationships through lies, you may need to have difficult conversations to rebuild trust. Restitution doesn't earn forgiveness, but it demonstrates sincere repentance and often brings additional healing to all parties involved.

Community plays a crucial role in healing from past mistakes. Dr. Curt Thompson notes that "healing is often a communal process, not a solitary one." Shame thrives in secrecy and isolation, but it cannot survive when exposed to light and love. Find safe relationships where you can share your struggles and receive encouragement, accountability, and prayer support. This might involve trusted friends, a pastor, a counselor, or a support group.

The practice of gratitude accelerates healing by shifting your focus from what you've done wrong to what God has done right. Instead of rehearsing failures, begin each day by thanking God for his forgiveness, his love, and his plans for your future. Gratitude doesn't deny reality, but it provides perspective that prevents past mistakes from overshadowing present blessings.

Remember that forgiveness isn't forgetting—it's remembering differently. You don't need to pretend your mistakes never happened, but you can remember them within the context of God's grace and redemption rather than condemnation and shame. This transformed memory becomes a source of humility, compassion for others, and deeper appreciation for God's mercy.

The ultimate goal of healing from past mistakes isn't to achieve a mistake-free life but to develop the resilience and wisdom that come from experiencing God's grace in the midst of failure. Your past mistakes, when surrendered to God, become part of your testimony and equip you to help others who are struggling with similar issues. Romans 8:28 promises that God works all things together for good for those who love him—even your worst mistakes can become part of his redemptive plan.

The Freedom of Forgiveness

True freedom comes not from the absence of problems but from the presence of forgiveness—both receiving it from God and extending it to others. Forgiveness is the key that unlocks every prison of resentment, bitterness, and condemnation, setting both the forgiver and the forgiven free to experience the abundant life Jesus promised. Understanding and practicing biblical forgiveness is essential for breaking free from guilt and shame because unforgiveness keeps us chained to our past while forgiveness opens the door to our future.

The foundation of all forgiveness is God's forgiveness toward us. The Bible teaches that we love because he first loved us, and we forgive because he first forgave us. Understanding the magnitude of

God's forgiveness—how much we've been forgiven—motivates and empowers us to extend that same forgiveness to others. When you truly grasp that you've been forgiven an unpayable debt, it becomes much easier to forgive the smaller debts others owe you.

God's forgiveness is both complete and unconditional. It's complete because Jesus paid the full penalty for all your sins—past, present, and future. There's nothing left for you to pay, no additional requirements to fulfill, no probationary period to complete. It's unconditional because it's based on God's character and Christ's work, not on your behavior or worthiness. This means you can't lose God's forgiveness by failing again, and you don't need to earn it by being good enough.

The scope of God's forgiveness is breathtaking. When Jesus died on the cross, he died for all your sins—all of them. There is nothing you have done or will do that wasn't covered on the cross. Colossians 2:13-14 says that God "forgave us all our sins, having canceled the charge of our legal indebtedness, which stood against us and condemned us; he has taken it away, nailing it to the cross." The word "all" doesn't leave room for exceptions.

Understanding God's forgiveness helps you grasp the true nature of forgiveness itself. Forgiveness is not excusing wrong behavior, pretending it didn't happen, or minimizing its impact. Forgiveness is choosing to release someone from the debt they owe you because of their wrongdoing. It's a decision to no longer hold their offense against them, even though they don't deserve that release. Forgiveness acknowledges that wrong was done but chooses mercy over justice.

The process of forgiving others begins with a decision, not a feeling. Forgiveness is an act of the will, not an emotion. You may not feel like forgiving, but you can choose to forgive because it's the right thing to do and because God commands it. The feelings often follow the decision, but waiting for feelings can leave you trapped in unforgiveness indefinitely. Jesus said to forgive "seventy-seven times" (Matthew 18:22), indicating that forgiveness is an ongoing choice, not a one-time event.

Forgiving others requires acknowledging the hurt they've caused you. This isn't about stuffing down emotions or pretending you weren't really injured. Forgiveness actually requires the opposite—it demands that you recognize and feel the pain so you can consciously choose to release it. Acknowledge the hurt, understand its impact on your life, and then make the deliberate choice to let it go. You can't forgive what you won't acknowledge.

The act of forgiveness involves several practical steps. First, identify specifically what you're forgiving—the particular actions, words, or failures that hurt you. Vague forgiveness isn't very effective; you need to name what you're releasing. Second, acknowledge the impact these actions had on your life, relationships, and emotional well-being. Third, choose to release your right to revenge, retaliation, or payment for what was done to you. Fourth, pray for the person who hurt you, asking God to bless them and work in their life.

Forgiveness doesn't necessarily mean reconciliation. Forgiveness is unilateral—you can forgive someone regardless of whether they acknowledge wrongdoing, apologize, or change their behavior.

Reconciliation, however, is bilateral and requires repentance, acknowledgment of wrongdoing, and often demonstrable change. You can forgive an abusive person while still maintaining appropriate boundaries to protect yourself from future harm.

The benefits of forgiveness extend far beyond the spiritual realm. Research shows that practicing forgiveness can improve mental and physical health, reduce stress and anxiety, lower blood pressure, and strengthen immune system function. Unforgiveness, by contrast, has been linked to depression, anxiety, heart disease, and compromised immune function. When you choose forgiveness, you're not just obeying God—you're protecting your own health and well-being.

Forgiveness is particularly powerful in breaking cycles of guilt and shame because it addresses both vertical and horizontal relationships. When you receive God's forgiveness, vertical healing occurs between you and God. When you extend forgiveness to others and receive their forgiveness, horizontal healing occurs in human relationships. Both dimensions are necessary for complete freedom from guilt and shame.

Self-forgiveness represents a crucial application of forgiveness principles. Many people find it easier to forgive others than to forgive themselves, but self-forgiveness is equally important for emotional and spiritual health. The same principles apply: acknowledge what you did wrong, understand its impact, choose to release yourself from ongoing self-punishment, and commit to making different choices in the future.

The practice of forgiveness requires spiritual strength that comes from the Holy Spirit. Humanly speaking, some offenses feel impossible to forgive—they're too painful, too devastating, or too personal. But with God's help, even the most difficult forgiveness becomes possible. The Holy Spirit provides both the desire to forgive and the power to follow through on that desire when your own strength is insufficient.

Forgiveness often needs to be repeated. You may forgive someone and then find yourself angry about the same situation later. This doesn't mean your original forgiveness was invalid—it means you need to choose forgiveness again. Like physical wounds that heal gradually, emotional wounds may require multiple applications of forgiveness before they're completely healed.

The ultimate model of forgiveness is Jesus himself, who forgave even while hanging on the cross: "Father, forgive them, for they do not know what they are doing" (Luke 23:34). Jesus forgave before anyone asked for forgiveness, before anyone acknowledged wrongdoing, and while the torture was still happening. This radical forgiveness demonstrates both the possibility and the power of choosing mercy over justice.

The freedom that comes from forgiveness affects every area of your life. It liberates mental and emotional energy that was being consumed by resentment and redirects it toward positive purposes. It opens your heart to deeper relationships and greater intimacy with God. It breaks generational cycles of bitterness that often pass from parents to children. Most importantly, it reflects God's character and draws others toward the hope and healing available in Christ.

Walking in Your New Identity

Perhaps the most transformative aspect of breaking free from guilt and shame is discovering and embracing your new identity in Christ. Most people live their entire lives based on false identities shaped by performance, past mistakes, other people's opinions, or worldly achievements. But when you become a Christian, God gives you a completely new identity that has nothing to do with your track record and everything to do with his love and grace. Learning to walk in this new identity is the key to permanent freedom from guilt and shame.

The biblical foundation for your new identity is found in 2 Corinthians 5:17: "Therefore, if anyone is in Christ, the new creation has come: The old has gone, the new is here!" This isn't metaphorical language—it's describing an actual spiritual transformation that occurs when you place your faith in Christ. You literally become a new creation, with a new nature, new potential, and new standing before God. The old you, with all its guilt and shame, has passed away.

Understanding regeneration is crucial for grasping your new identity. Regeneration means spiritual rebirth—you've been born again into God's family with a completely new spiritual DNA. Just as physical birth gives you genetic characteristics from your earthly parents, spiritual rebirth gives you spiritual characteristics from your heavenly Father. You now share God's nature, inherit his promises, and possess his righteousness as your own.

Your new identity includes multiple biblical designations that completely redefine who you are. You are God's beloved child (1 John 3:1), his friend (John 15:15), his bride (Ephesians 5:25-27), his ambassador (2 Corinthians 5:20), his temple (1 Corinthians 6:19), his workmanship (Ephesians 2:10), and his chosen possession (1 Peter 2:9). Each of these identities carries profound implications for how you view yourself and how you should expect to be treated by others.

The process of walking in your new identity begins with renewing your mind to align with God's truth about who you are. Romans 12:2 instructs us to "be transformed by the renewing of your mind." This renewal involves replacing old thought patterns based on false identities with new thought patterns based on your identity in Christ. When shame whispers, "You're worthless," you respond with, "I am God's beloved child." When guilt declares, "You're a failure," you counter with, "I am God's workmanship, created for good works."

Your new identity is not based on your performance but on Christ's performance. This is perhaps the most liberating truth in all of Scripture. Your standing before God doesn't fluctuate based on your behavior, emotions, or circumstances. It's permanently established by what Jesus accomplished on the cross. You are as loved on your worst day as you are on your best day because God's love is based on Christ's perfect record, not your imperfect one.

The practical implications of your new identity are staggering. It means you can approach God with confidence, knowing you're not just tolerated but welcomed as a beloved family member. It means you have direct access to the throne room of heaven without needing to grovel or earn your way in. It means you carry the presence and power of God wherever you go because you are his temple. It means you have a purpose and calling that transcends your natural abilities or past failures.

Walking in your new identity requires both understanding and application. Understanding involves studying what Scripture says about who you are in Christ, meditating on these truths, and memorizing key verses that affirm your identity. Application involves acting on these truths even when you don't feel them, making decisions based on your true identity rather than your emotions, and treating yourself with the dignity that befits a child of God.

One of the biggest obstacles to walking in your new identity is the tendency to focus on your old identity when you fail or struggle. When you sin, your flesh wants to return to shame-based thinking: "I'm such a failure," "I'll never change," "God must be disappointed in me." Your new identity in Christ provides a different perspective: "I'm a righteous person who occasionally acts unrighteously," "God's love for me never changes," "This failure doesn't define me because Christ defines me."

The practice of identity-based decision making revolutionizes how you live. Instead of asking, "What do I want to do?" or "What do I feel like doing?" you ask, "What would someone with my identity in Christ do in this situation?" This approach aligns your behavior with your true identity rather than with your fluctuating emotions or circumstances. It's incredibly powerful for breaking negative behavior patterns that stem from false identities.

Your new identity also affects how you relate to others. When you know you're loved, accepted, and secure in Christ, you don't need to derive your worth from other people's approval or performance. This freedom allows you to love others without conditions, serve without keeping score, and forgive without bitterness. You can afford to be generous with grace because you know your own tank is always full.

The enemy's primary strategy against your new identity is to convince you to live according to your old identity. He'll remind you of past failures, highlight current struggles, and compare you unfavorably to others. But these attacks lose their power when you're grounded in the truth of who God says you are. When the enemy accuses, you can respond with confidence: "I hear your accusations, but I know who I am in Christ, and your voice carries no weight in my life."

Community plays a vital role in helping you walk in your new identity. Surround yourself with people who know your true identity and will remind you of it when you forget. Choose friends, mentors, and church communities that speak truth about who you are in Christ rather than reinforcing shame-based thinking. Allow others to see your true self without the masks that shame demands you wear.

The transformation from old identity to new identity is often gradual. While your spiritual standing changes instantly at salvation, renewing your mind and emotions to align with this new reality takes time. Be patient with yourself during this process. Every time you choose to believe God's truth about your identity over the lies of guilt and shame, you're building new neural pathways that will eventually make identity-based thinking more natural.

Your new identity becomes most visible during times of trial and failure. This is when your true beliefs about yourself are tested. Do you retreat into shame and self-condemnation, or do you stand firm in your identity as God's beloved child? These moments provide opportunities to demonstrate the transforming power of your new identity not just to others but to yourself.

The ultimate goal of walking in your new identity isn't personal happiness or self-esteem—it's bringing glory to God by living as he designed you to live. When you walk confidently in your identity as his child, you display his character to a watching world. You demonstrate that God's love is powerful enough to transform lives, heal wounds, and create new beginnings. Your freedom from guilt and shame becomes a testimony to the redemptive power of the Gospel and an invitation for others to discover their own new identity in Christ.

CHAPTER 9: OVERCOMING DEPRESSION AND DESPAIR

Sarah stared at the ceiling for what felt like hours, though the clock revealed it had only been twenty minutes since she'd woken up. The familiar weight settled on her chest—that crushing sensation that made even breathing feel like work. Another day stretched ahead of her, filled with responsibilities she felt too exhausted to meet and people she felt too broken to face. Her mind, once her ally, had become her greatest enemy, firing a relentless barrage of criticism and hopelessness that seemed to drown out any possibility of joy or peace. She wondered if this was just who she was now—if the vibrant, hopeful person she used to be was gone forever.

If Sarah's experience resonates with you, you're not alone in this battle. Recent research from Stanford Medicine shows that depression affects brain circuitry in measurable ways, but crucially, that these changes can be reversed through therapeutic intervention. The journey from despair to hope isn't about simply "thinking positive" or "snapping out of it"—it's about understanding how depression hijacks our mental processes and learning specific, science-backed strategies to reclaim control. What Sarah didn't realize in that dark moment was that her mind, despite feeling like her enemy, actually contained all the tools necessary for her recovery. The same brain that was generating hopeless thoughts had the capacity to generate hope, create momentum, and find genuine light in even the darkest circumstances. This chapter will show you exactly how to activate that capacity, drawing from cutting-edge research in cognitive behavioral therapy, hope theory, and behavioral activation to give you a roadmap out of depression's grip.

When Your Mind Feels Hijacked

Depression doesn't just change how you feel—it fundamentally alters how your brain processes information, making thoughts that would normally seem unreasonable appear absolutely true. Cognitive behavioral therapy research has identified specific patterns called "cognitive distortions" that become dominant during depressive episodes, including all-or-nothing thinking, fortune-telling, and mental filtering. These distortions work like a hacker infiltrating your mental operating system, causing you to interpret neutral or even positive events through a lens of negativity and hopelessness.

When your mind feels hijacked by depression, you're experiencing what researchers call the "negative cognitive triad"—a systematic distortion of how you view yourself, the world, and your future. According to Beck's foundational research, this triad manifests as "I am worthless" (negative view of self), "The world is hostile" (negative view of environment), and "Nothing will ever change" (negative view of future). Understanding this pattern is crucial because it helps you recognize that these thoughts aren't facts—they're symptoms of a hijacked thought process.

The hijacking happens gradually, often so subtly that you don't notice until you're already deep in depression's grip. Your brain begins to develop what scientists call "automatic negative thoughts"—those instant, reflexive judgments that pop up in response to everyday situations. These automatic thoughts both trigger and enhance depression, creating a self-reinforcing cycle where negative thinking generates negative emotions, which then generate more negative thinking. For instance, when you wake up feeling tired, instead of thinking "I had a restless night," your hijacked mind immediately jumps to "I'm always exhausted because I'm weak and can't handle life."

Stanford Medicine's latest research reveals something remarkable about this hijacking process: it creates measurable changes in brain circuitry, but these changes are reversible when addressed with proper therapeutic techniques. This means that what feels like a permanent alteration of your personality is actually a temporary disruption that can be corrected. The key is learning to catch the hijacking in action and implement specific countermeasures.

One of the most insidious aspects of mental hijacking is how it affects your perception of time and possibility. Depression compresses your timeline, making temporary difficulties feel permanent and making it impossible to imagine that things could ever be different. Common cognitive distortions include "fortune-telling" (predicting negative outcomes without considering alternatives) and "magnifying" (making bigger deals about specific negative events). When you're late to work, your hijacked mind doesn't just see an inconvenient morning—it sees evidence that you're irresponsible, that your boss will fire you, and that you'll never be able to maintain employment.

The hijacking also affects what psychologists call your "attention bias." Instead of noticing the full spectrum of your daily experiences, your depressed brain develops tunnel vision, zeroing in on anything that confirms your negative beliefs while filtering out contradictory evidence. This mental filtering means "picking out a single negative detail and dwelling on it exclusively so that the vision of reality becomes darkened". If you receive ten positive comments and one criticism, your hijacked mind will dismiss the positives and fixate on the negative feedback as proof of your inadequacy.

Breaking free from this hijacking requires what researchers call "metacognitive awareness"—the ability to think about your thinking. Cognitive behavioral therapy teaches patients to examine their thought processes systematically, rating both the intensity of emotions and the believability of thoughts on scales from 0-100. This isn't about forcing positivity but about developing the skill to observe your thoughts objectively, like a scientist studying data rather than a victim drowning in emotion.

The process begins with learning to identify "trigger moments"—those specific instances when your emotional state shifts dramatically. Effective cognitive behavioral therapy teaches patients to record upsetting incidents as soon as possible after they occur, noting the specific thoughts, emotions, and physical sensations present. Maybe it's receiving a text message, looking in the mirror, or remembering a conversation from earlier. These moments reveal the automatic thoughts that are driving your emotional responses.

Once you can identify these automatic thoughts, you can begin testing their validity. Depression's hijacking makes thoughts feel absolutely true, but reality is often much more nuanced. Research shows that challenging these thoughts through "guided discovery" helps patients recognize the difference between thoughts and facts. Instead of accepting "I always mess everything up" as gospel truth, you can ask yourself: Is this always true? What evidence supports this? What evidence contradicts it? What would I tell a friend who had this thought?

The hijacking metaphor is particularly helpful because it reminds you that this isn't your true self talking—it's depression's voice masquerading as your own thoughts. Cognitive behavioral theory suggests that depression results from "maladaptive, faulty, or irrational cognitions taking the form of distorted thoughts, core beliefs, and judgments". Recognizing this distinction is the first step toward reclaiming your mental sovereignty. Your real self is the observer who can notice these distorted thoughts, question their validity, and choose different responses.

Hope as a Powerful Weapon

Hope isn't just a feel-good emotion—it's a scientifically validated psychological weapon against depression that works by restructuring how your brain processes goals and possibilities. Research shows that hope consists of two cognitive components: agency thinking (the belief that you can achieve your goals) and pathways thinking (the ability to identify specific routes to reach those goals). When depression hijacks your mind, it systematically attacks both components, making you feel powerless (low agency) and stuck (limited pathways). Understanding how to rebuild hope through both components gives you a strategic advantage in your recovery.

Meta-analytic research demonstrates that higher levels of both agency and pathways thinking are associated with significantly less depression and anxiety, with agency thinking showing particularly strong protective effects. This isn't coincidental—hope directly counteracts depression's core lies. When depression tells you "nothing you do matters," agency thinking responds with "my actions have impact." When depression insists "there's no way out," pathways thinking generates multiple routes forward.

The weaponization of hope begins with understanding its neurological foundation. Studies of cognitive behavior therapy show that hope operates as a transdiagnostic mechanism of change, meaning it facilitates recovery across different types of mental health challenges. When you cultivate hope, you're not just changing your emotions—you're rewiring neural pathways that had been dominated by depression's narrative of helplessness and hopelessness.

Agency thinking—your belief in your ability to pursue goals—is particularly powerful because it directly challenges depression's lies about your capability and worth. Research indicates that agency thinking becomes more important with age and shows stronger associations with depression reduction than pathways thinking. This makes sense when you consider that depression often begins with a sense of powerlessness. Building agency starts with recognizing moments when you do have control, however small they might seem.

The cultivation of agency thinking requires what researchers call "mastery experiences"—situations where you successfully accomplish something meaningful to you. Behavioral activation research emphasizes starting with activities that are both easy to accomplish and personally rewarding, creating a foundation for building confidence. This might mean setting a goal to walk around the block, call one friend, or organize a single drawer. Each small success provides evidence against depression's claims about your incompetence, gradually rebuilding your sense of personal agency.

Pathways thinking—your ability to identify multiple routes to your goals—serves as hope's strategic component. Hope therapy specifically teaches individuals to generate alternative pathways when obstacles arise, helping them develop mental flexibility that depression typically destroys. Depression creates tunnel vision, making it impossible to see options that are actually available. Pathways thinking deliberately widens your perspective, helping you brainstorm multiple approaches to challenges.

The development of pathways thinking often requires external support initially, as depression can severely limit your ability to see options independently. Research on hope as a mechanism of change shows that therapeutic environments can help individuals identify pathways they couldn't see on their own. This is why talking through problems with trusted friends, family members, or counselors can be so powerful—they can help you map routes that depression has hidden from your view.

Studies demonstrate that hope and forgiveness work together to reduce depression, with forgiveness serving as a mediator between basic hope and reduced depressive symptoms. This connection reveals an important aspect of hope as a weapon: it often requires releasing resentment and self-condemnation that feed depression's narrative. Forgiveness—of yourself and others—clears space for

145

hope to grow by removing the emotional debris that blocks pathways to healing.

The strategic deployment of hope involves what researchers call "hope enhancement interventions." Meta-analytic research on hope enhancement strategies shows that while these interventions are moderately effective, they work best when combined with other therapeutic approaches. This suggests that hope isn't meant to be your only weapon but rather the foundation that makes other recovery strategies more effective.

One of hope's most powerful mechanisms is its ability to interrupt rumination—that endless cycle of negative thinking that characterizes depression. Research on individuals with schizophrenia and depression shows that hope mediates the relationship between depression and recovery, helping break cycles of negative thinking. When you're actively engaged in agency and pathways thinking, your mind has less capacity for rumination because it's focused on constructive problem-solving rather than destructive self-criticism.

Hope also works by changing your relationship with time. Depression compresses your timeline, making current pain feel eternal and making it impossible to imagine a different future. Research on positive mental health shows that hope promotes well-being more effectively than optimism or self-efficacy alone. Unlike simple optimism (expecting good things to happen), hope is active—it involves identifying specific goals and developing concrete plans to achieve them.

The practical application of hope as a weapon requires daily cultivation through what researchers call "hope behaviors." Studies show that individuals with higher hope demonstrate better treatment continuance and play more active roles in their own recovery from both physical and mental illness. This might involve writing down three specific goals each morning, identifying at least two pathways to achieve each goal, and taking one concrete action step toward your most important objective.

Creating Mental Momentum

Mental momentum operates on the same principle as physical momentum—small movements in the right direction can gradually build into unstoppable force that carries you toward recovery. Psychological momentum research shows that sequential runs of success create "a psychological force in which several factors converge synergistically to enable performance at levels not ordinarily possible". In depression recovery, this means that tiny positive actions can compound over time, creating an upward spiral that becomes increasingly difficult for depression to disrupt.

The foundation of mental momentum lies in understanding what researchers call "behavioral activation"—the strategic use of activity to influence mood and thinking. Behavioral activation research demonstrates that by deliberately practicing certain behaviors, people can "activate" positive emotional states, making them more likely to continue participating in beneficial activities. This challenges depression's central lie that you need to feel better before you can act better. In reality, action often precedes motivation, not the other way around.

Studies show that there's a close relationship between activity levels and mood—when we feel good, we naturally engage in rewarding activities, which creates positive feedback effects through pleasure, mastery, and connection. Depression disrupts this natural cycle by reducing activity levels, which decreases opportunities for positive experiences, which further lowers mood in a vicious downward spiral. Creating mental momentum means deliberately reversing this cycle by increasing activity even when motivation is low.

The process begins with activity monitoring—systematically tracking what you do and how you feel to identify patterns between your behavior and mood. Behavioral activation therapy teaches individuals to record activities for each waking hour and rate their mood on a 0-10 scale, revealing connections they might not have noticed. You might discover that phone calls with certain friends consistently improve your mood, while scrolling social media reliably makes you feel worse. This data becomes the foundation for strategic momentum-building.

The key to sustainable momentum is starting with what researchers call "low-threshold activities"—actions that require minimal energy and have high probability of success. Behavioral activation emphasizes beginning with activities that are easy to accomplish, require minimal resources, and can be completed in short amounts of time. This might mean taking a five-minute walk instead of committing to an hour at the gym, or sending one encouraging text message instead of trying to socialize for an entire evening.

Research shows that over the course of a few weeks of behavioral activation, people start to feel noticeably better as they get the ball rolling and pick up momentum that feeds back into more energy and motivation. This creates what psychologists call a "positive feedback loop"—small actions lead to slight mood improvements, which provide energy for slightly bigger actions, which create more significant mood improvements, and so on. The momentum builds on itself naturally once you provide the initial push.

The concept of "small wins" is crucial for understanding how mental momentum operates. Research on behavioral activation with children emphasizes celebrating small wins to maintain motivation and continue the activation process. Each completed task, no matter how minor it might seem, provides evidence against depression's narrative of incompetence and helplessness. When you successfully make your bed, respond to an email, or prepare a healthy meal, you're proving to yourself that you're capable of positive action.

Momentum requires strategic planning rather than random activity. Behavioral activation therapy emphasizes structured planning that specifies exactly what will be done, when and where activities will occur, and how they fit into a client's daily schedule. This planning process prevents the decision fatigue that often derails good intentions. Instead of hoping you'll "do something productive today," you commit to specific actions at specific times, removing the mental energy required to make these decisions in the moment.

One of the most powerful aspects of mental momentum is how it changes your relationship with setbacks. Psychological momentum research shows that early successes can create lasting positive effects that persist even when temporary obstacles arise. Once you've experienced the reality of positive change through your own actions, isolated bad days feel like temporary setbacks rather than evidence that you're doomed to permanent suffering.

The momentum principle also applies to cognitive change. Research demonstrates that behavioral activation is often as effective as cognitive therapy alone, and sometimes more effective, because changing behavior naturally leads to changes in thoughts and feelings. When you act like someone who has energy and purpose, your mind begins to generate thoughts consistent with that identity. This is why "fake it till you make it" can actually be scientifically sound advice when applied strategically.

Creating sustainable momentum requires attention to what researchers call "reinforcement schedules." Behavioral activation emphasizes increasing positive reinforcement while ending negative behavior patterns that maintain depression. This means not only adding beneficial activities but also gradually reducing behaviors that provide temporary relief but ultimately worsen depression— like excessive sleeping, social isolation, or endless social media scrolling.

The social component of momentum cannot be overlooked. Research emphasizes building support systems as vital for maintaining momentum, as healthy relationships provide both accountability and positive reinforcement for recovery efforts. Sharing your goals with trusted friends or family members creates external motivation that can carry you through periods when internal motivation falters.

Advanced momentum building involves what researchers call "values-based activation"—ensuring that your activities align with what you genuinely care about rather than what you think you should do. Behavioral activation therapy emphasizes identifying personal values and goals to ensure that activities feel meaningful rather than like arbitrary assignments. When your actions connect to your deeper purposes, they generate more sustained motivation and create momentum that feels authentic rather than forced.

Finding Light in the Darkness

Finding light in darkness isn't about pretending the darkness doesn't exist or forcing artificial positivity—it's about developing the skills to perceive and cultivate genuine sources of hope, meaning, and growth even in the midst of profound suffering. Recent research on depression recovery emphasizes that finding light involves learning to navigate emotions skillfully while rebuilding strength and emerging resilient. This process requires both practical strategies and a fundamental shift in how you relate to difficult experiences.

The metaphor of light in darkness is particularly apt for depression recovery because it acknowledges both the reality of suffering and the possibility of transformation. Depression often feels like being trapped in a windowless room, convinced that no light exists anywhere. But learning to find light doesn't mean the room suddenly becomes sunny—it means developing the ability to strike matches, find candles, and eventually locate the door. The darkness remains real, but it no longer has absolute power over your experience.

One of the most powerful ways to find light is through what researchers call "meaning-making"—the human capacity to derive purpose and significance from even painful experiences. Studies on positive psychology and recovery show that individuals who can find meaning in their struggles often experience what's called "post-traumatic growth"—actual psychological improvement beyond their pre-crisis levels. This doesn't mean you should be grateful for depression, but it does mean you can potentially use this experience to develop wisdom, empathy, and resilience you might never have gained otherwise.

The process of meaning-making often begins with reframing your depression story. Instead of seeing yourself as a victim of a cruel disease, you can begin to view yourself as someone engaged in a heroic journey of healing and growth. Depression counseling research emphasizes that therapy provides a space to explore underlying issues and reconstruct a more balanced emotional landscape. This reframing doesn't minimize your suffering but places it in a larger context where pain can serve a purpose and growth becomes possible.

Finding light also involves developing what psychologists call "present-moment awareness"—the ability to notice positive elements in your current experience even when your overall mood is low. Mindfulness research shows that depression often involves being caught up in thinking about the past or worrying about the future, preventing people from fully experiencing what they're actually doing. When you learn to focus attention on immediate sensory experiences—the warmth of sunlight, the taste of coffee, the texture of fabric—you often discover that the present moment contains more neutrality or even pleasantness than your depressed thoughts would suggest.

The cultivation of present-moment awareness requires practice because depression trains your mind to automatically scan for problems and threats. Mindfulness-based approaches to depression help individuals recognize what their minds are telling them without automatically believing every thought. This creates space between you and your depressive thoughts, allowing you to observe them with curiosity rather than being overwhelmed by them.

Another pathway to light involves recognizing and nurturing what researchers call "positive resources." Studies show that enhancing positive psychological resources helps individuals overcome adversity and cope with stress more effectively. These resources might include gratitude practices, acts of kindness, creative expression, spiritual practices, or connection with nature. The key is finding resources that genuinely resonate with you rather than forcing yourself into practices that feel inauthentic.

The social dimension of finding light cannot be understated. Research emphasizes that building and maintaining healthy relationships provides crucial glimmers of hope amid depression's darkness. Sometimes light comes through the care of others—a friend's understanding text message, a family member's patience, or a therapist's steady presence. Learning to receive this light from others, even when you can't generate it internally, becomes a crucial skill in recovery.

Finding light often involves rediscovering activities and experiences that once brought you joy. Depression counseling approaches include structured planning to reintroduce meaningful activities and create positive triggers that foster both joy and patience. This might mean returning to creative hobbies, reconnecting with nature, listening to music that moves you, or engaging with books, movies, or art that inspire hope. The goal isn't to recapture exactly who you used to be but to discover who you're becoming through this process of healing.

The journey toward light also requires what researchers call "self-compassion"—treating yourself with the same kindness you would show a good friend going through difficult times. Recovery research emphasizes that self-care isn't selfish but necessary for the healing journey. This involves speaking to yourself gently, acknowledging your efforts even when results aren't immediately visible, and recognizing that healing is not linear but involves setbacks and breakthroughs in unpredictable patterns.

One of the most profound sources of light comes from helping others who are struggling. Research on recovery shows that individuals who engage in altruistic activities often experience significant improvements in their own mental health. This doesn't mean you should neglect your own healing to focus on others, but rather that small acts of kindness—sending encouraging messages, volunteering for causes you care about, or simply being present for someone else's pain—can generate meaning and purpose that depression cannot easily extinguish.

The process of finding light requires patience because it often happens gradually rather than dramatically. Recovery research indicates that finding light in darkness is a gradual process that requires consistent application of helpful strategies. Some days you might only perceive a tiny flicker of hope or meaning. Other days the light might feel stronger and more sustained. The key is learning to notice and appreciate whatever light is available rather than dismissing it because it's not as bright as you wish it were.

Finding light ultimately involves developing what researchers call "resilience"—not the ability to avoid being affected by difficulty, but the capacity to navigate challenges while maintaining some sense of hope and possibility. Clinical psychology research shows that individuals can learn to rebuild strength and emerge resilient from even severe mental health challenges. This resilience doesn't mean you'll never struggle again, but it does mean you'll have tools and perspectives that allow you to find your way back to light even when darkness returns.

The light you find in darkness often becomes a permanent part of who you are—a source of strength you can access not only for your own healing but also to help illuminate the path for others who are still struggling. Recovery research emphasizes that individuals who successfully navigate depression often develop profound levels of compassion and insight that serve them throughout their lives. The very experience that once felt like pure darkness can become a source of wisdom, empathy, and hope that enriches not only your own life but the lives of everyone you encounter on your continued journey toward wholeness.

CHAPTER 10: SILENCING THE INNER CRITIC

Marcus had just finished giving what he thought was a successful presentation at work when the familiar voice started whispering in his ear. "You stumbled over that one section," it hissed. "Did you see how Jennifer looked when you mentioned the budget? She thinks you're incompetent. Everyone in that room knows you don't belong here." By the time he reached his car, the voice had constructed an elaborate narrative about how his colleagues were probably already discussing his inadequacies and how his boss was reconsidering his promotion. This wasn't the voice of a colleague or supervisor—it was coming from inside his own mind, and it had been his constant companion for as long as he could remember.

The inner critic is perhaps the most relentless opponent you'll face in your journey toward mental freedom. Unlike external critics, who eventually go home or move on with their lives, your inner critic travels with you everywhere, offering a running commentary on your performance, appearance, decisions, and worth as a human being. Recent research shows that six main types of self-critic emerge in adults: Teamster, Non-feeler, Worrier, Not good enough for self, Not good enough for others, and Hated self. Understanding which type of inner critic dominates your mental landscape is crucial because achieving self-integrity requires eliciting self-compassionate and self-protective strategies to process the internal monologue relating to various self-critics. This chapter will show you how to identify your specific inner critic patterns, neutralize their power, and replace that harsh internal voice with one that speaks life, hope, and truth over your future. The goal isn't to eliminate all self-evaluation—healthy self-reflection serves important purposes—but to silence the destructive voice that masquerades as wisdom while actually sabotaging your growth and happiness.

The Voice of Self-Condemnation

The inner critic is not your friend, despite its claims to be helping you improve or protecting you from failure. The roots of our inner critics are found in childhood, where the founding father of psychoanalysis, Sigmund Freud, explained the formation of our superegos as a process during which we internalize external views of ourselves—predominantly those of our parents. What begins as external criticism from caregivers, teachers, or peers becomes internalized and automated, creating a relentless internal voice that continues the criticism long after the original critics have disappeared from our lives.

Understanding the voice of self-condemnation requires recognizing its fundamental characteristics and distinguishing it from healthy self-reflection. The inner critic often manifests as negative self-talk, self-doubt, and feelings of inadequacy, significantly impacting mental health and well-being by leading to high levels of anxiety, low self-esteem, and even depression. The inner critic doesn't offer constructive feedback aimed at genuine improvement—instead, it delivers harsh judgments designed to make you feel fundamentally flawed and unworthy.

The voice of self-condemnation has several distinctive features that separate it from helpful self-evaluation. First, it operates in absolutes. Where healthy self-reflection might observe "I made a mistake in that presentation," the inner critic declares "You always mess everything up" or "You're completely incompetent." This all-or-nothing thinking creates a cognitive distortion that makes normal human errors feel like evidence of total inadequacy. The inner critic specializes in words like "always," "never," "completely," and "totally," transforming specific incidents into character indictments.

Second, the inner critic uses a tone and language that you would never accept from another person. When you're self-critical, you might want to notice what words you actually use—are there key phrases that come up over and over again? What is the tone of your voice—harsh, cold, angry? Does the voice remind you of anyone in your past who was critical of you? Many people report that their inner critic uses phrases like "You're so stupid," "What's wrong with you?" or "You're pathetic"—language that would be considered verbal abuse if spoken by someone else but somehow seems acceptable when it comes from within.

Third, the voice of self-condemnation has an uncanny ability to find fault in any situation. When you succeed, it minimizes the achievement ("Anyone could have done that") or predicts future failure ("You just got lucky this time"). When you fail, it uses the experience as evidence of your fundamental unworthiness ("See? I told you that you couldn't do it"). This creates what psychologists call a "no-win scenario" where the inner critic maintains its narrative regardless of actual outcomes.

The development of this condemning voice typically occurs during critical developmental periods. The prefrontal cortex, the part of the brain responsible for decision-making and emotional regulation, isn't fully developed until age twenty-five. If individuals constantly hear harsh criticism during this critical developmental period, it can lead them to adopt negative beliefs about themselves and harbor self-doubt. This explains why many adults carry voices that sound remarkably like critical parents, teachers, or other authority figures from their childhood.

The neurological basis of the inner critic reveals why it can feel so automatic and persistent. Self-criticism is a crucial factor in generating negative emotions, including shame, while research shows that self-compassion and self-forgiveness can mitigate the effects of self-criticism and shame. When the inner critic activates, it triggers stress responses in the brain that can actually impair cognitive function, making it harder to think clearly and solve problems effectively.

Understanding the specific tactics of self-condemnation helps you recognize when it's operating. The inner critic often uses temporal distortions, taking past mistakes and projecting them infinitely into the future ("You'll never be able to maintain a relationship"). It engages in mind reading, assuming it knows what others are thinking ("Everyone thinks you're boring"). It uses emotional reasoning, treating feelings as facts ("I feel like a failure, therefore I am a failure").

One of the most insidious aspects of the condemning voice is how it masquerades as motivation or protection. The inner critic often justifies its harsh treatment by claiming it's pushing you to be better or protecting you from disappointment. "If I don't criticize myself, I'll get lazy" or "If I expect the worst, I won't be disappointed" are common rationalizations. However, research consistently shows that self-criticism is less effective than self-compassion for motivation and personal growth.

The voice of self-condemnation also exhibits a peculiar relationship with success and happiness. Rather than celebrating achievements, it immediately shifts focus to what's next or what could go wrong. This prevents you from experiencing satisfaction or building confidence from your accomplishments. The inner critic seems to operate under the assumption that feeling good about yourself is dangerous and must be prevented at all costs.

Recognizing the voice of self-condemnation is the first step toward silencing it. By recognizing that you house an inner critic, you are taking the extremely important step of seeing that part of you is a critic, making clear that part of you is being victimized by that critic. Inherent in this perspective is that there is a third part of you who is an observer, seeing the dynamic between those two. This observing self—the part of you that can notice and evaluate your thoughts—is where your power to change lies.

The condemning voice often becomes so familiar that it feels like your own thoughts, but it's crucial to understand that these thoughts are not facts about you—they're simply neural patterns that have become habituated through repetition. Participants in self-compassion interventions learn to become more aware of their inner self-critique and develop kinder attitudes toward themselves. This awareness creates the space necessary for transformation, allowing you to respond to the inner critic rather than automatically believing everything it says.

Replacing Negative Self-Talk

Replacing negative self-talk is not about forcing artificial positivity or pretending problems don't exist—it's about developing more accurate, balanced, and helpful ways of thinking about yourself and your experiences. Cognitive restructuring helps individuals recognize when they are getting stuck in distorted patterns of thinking (identifying thinking traps) and come up with new ways to think about their situation (writing reframed thoughts). The process involves identifying negative thought patterns, evaluating their accuracy and helpfulness, and consciously choosing more constructive alternatives.

The foundation of replacing negative self-talk lies in understanding cognitive distortions—systematic errors in thinking that the inner critic loves to employ. Cognitive restructuring helps clients discover, challenge, and modify or replace their negative, irrational thoughts (or cognitive distortions). Common distortions include catastrophizing (imagining the worst possible outcome), all-or-nothing thinking (seeing situations in only two categories), mental filtering (focusing exclusively on negative details), and personalization (taking responsibility for things beyond your control).

The process begins with developing awareness of your specific negative self-talk patterns. The first step towards changing how you treat yourself is to notice when you are being self-critical. Whenever you're feeling bad about something, think about what you've just said to yourself. Try to be as accurate as possible, noting your inner speech verbatim. This awareness stage is crucial because many people have lived with negative self-talk for so long that it has become background noise—present but not consciously noticed.

Once you've identified specific negative thoughts, the next step involves examining their accuracy and utility. Effective techniques for cognitive restructuring include Socratic questioning, thought records, and behavioral experiments, which empower individuals to challenge irrational beliefs and foster more balanced thinking. Socratic questioning involves asking yourself: "Is this thought absolutely true?" "What evidence supports this thought?" "What evidence contradicts it?" "How might someone else view this situation?" "What would I tell a good friend who had this thought?"

Thought records provide a structured way to track and analyze negative self-talk. A popular thought record instructs you to record the situation, thoughts, emotions, behaviors, and alternate thought. For example, if you make a mistake at work, you might record: Situation—Made error in report; Thought—"I'm terrible at my job"; Emotion—Shame, anxiety; Behavior—Avoided colleagues; Alternate thought—"I made a mistake, which is normal. I can learn from this and do better next time."

The goal of replacing negative self-talk is not to eliminate all critical thinking but to develop what researchers call "realistic optimism"—thinking that is both accurate and helpful. Cognitive restructuring is not just about positive thinking; it encourages realistic and balanced thinking, contributing to overall mental well-being. This means acknowledging real problems while avoiding catastrophic interpretations and recognizing strengths while maintaining motivation for growth.

Research on cognitive restructuring reveals its neurological benefits. Studies using functional magnetic resonance imaging show that positive self-talk interventions modulate connectivity among motivation-related regions, including the nucleus accumbens, while negative self-talk changes the wide range of self-referential, default mode, and reward-motivation networks. This suggests that deliberately practicing positive self-talk literally rewires your brain, making constructive thinking more automatic over time.

One effective technique for replacing negative self-talk is the "friend perspective" method. If you're having trouble thinking of what words to use, you might want to imagine what a very compassionate friend would say to you in this situation. Most people find it much easier to speak kindly to others than to themselves. By imagining how you would comfort a friend facing the same situation, you can access more balanced and compassionate language for your internal dialogue.

Another powerful approach involves temporal reframing—expanding your time perspective beyond the immediate situation. Cognitive reframing is a psychological technique aimed at helping individuals modify their perspective on challenging situations, encouraging a shift from negative to more neutral or positive interpretations. When you're caught in negative self-talk about a current problem, ask yourself: "How much will this matter in five years?" "What have I learned from similar situations in the past?" "How have I grown from previous challenges?"

The practice of replacing negative self-talk also involves developing what psychologists call "implementation intentions"—specific if-then plans for handling negative thoughts. For example: "If I notice myself thinking 'I'm so stupid,' then I will pause and ask 'What

163

would be a more accurate and helpful way to think about this?'" This pre-planning helps override automatic negative responses with more constructive alternatives.

Behavioral experiments provide another avenue for challenging negative self-talk. Cognitive restructuring for people with depression has positive effects, as it aims to modify the behavioral response, changing automatic thinking and consequent emotions, creating alternative behavioral responses. If your inner critic claims "No one wants to hear what you have to say," you might test this belief by speaking up in a meeting and observing the actual response rather than assuming the worst.

The replacement process requires patience and persistence. This exercise should be done over several weeks and will eventually form the blueprint for changing how you relate to yourself long-term. Negative self-talk patterns typically develop over years or decades, so transformation doesn't happen overnight. However, research shows that consistent practice in cognitive restructuring leads to measurable improvements in mood, self-esteem, and overall mental health.

It's important to approach this work with self-compassion rather than self-criticism. Many people become frustrated when they notice themselves falling back into negative self-talk patterns, but this frustration simply creates another layer of self-criticism. Instead, treat each moment of awareness as a victory—every time you notice negative self-talk, you're creating an opportunity for change.

Building Healthy Self-Worth

Building healthy self-worth is fundamentally different from inflating your ego or developing narcissistic tendencies. Research shows that high self-esteem is distinct from narcissism—whereas self-esteem refers to feelings of self-acceptance and self-respect, narcissism is characterized by feelings of superiority, grandiosity, entitlement and self-centeredness. Healthy self-worth involves developing a stable, realistic appreciation for your inherent value as a human being, independent of your achievements, appearance, or approval from others.

The foundation of healthy self-worth rests on understanding the difference between conditional and unconditional self-regard. Conditional self-worth depends on meeting certain standards—getting good grades, achieving career success, maintaining a particular appearance, or receiving approval from specific people. People who experience a steady diet of disapproval from important others—family, supervisors, friends, teachers—might have feelings of low self-esteem. This creates a fragile sense of worth that fluctuates based on external circumstances and performance.

Unconditional self-worth, by contrast, recognizes your fundamental value as a human being regardless of your achievements or failures. This doesn't mean believing you're perfect or better than others—it means accepting that your core worth is not determined by your performance. No one person is less worthy than the next person, and no one is deemed more important. Knowing this detail is crucial. This perspective provides a stable foundation that can weather setbacks, criticism, and failures without devastating your sense of self.

Research on self-esteem development reveals that healthy self-worth involves multiple components working together. Self-esteem works at two different levels—our overall self-worth (global) and how we rate ourselves in specific areas like academics or appearance. Additionally, trait self-esteem stays stable across situations, while state self-esteem changes based on recent experiences and social feedback. Building healthy self-worth requires attention to both global self-acceptance and realistic confidence in specific domains.

One of the most effective approaches to building healthy self-worth involves developing self-compassion—treating yourself with the same kindness and understanding you would show a good friend facing difficulties. Kristin Neff, a professor of Psychology at the University of Texas, identifies three primary components of self-compassion: Self-kindness (treating yourself with kindness when confronted with pain rather than engaging in self-criticism), Common humanity (acknowledging that challenges and personal failure are normal aspects of human experience), and Mindfulness (maintaining awareness of your experience without being overwhelmed by it).

Self-kindness involves speaking to yourself with gentleness, especially during difficult times. Instead of berating yourself for mistakes, you learn to offer yourself the same comfort and encouragement you would give to someone you care about. This might mean saying, "This is really hard right now, and it's understandable that I'm struggling" instead of "I should be able to handle this better."

The common humanity component helps combat the isolation and shame that often accompany personal struggles. Self-compassion involves acknowledging that challenges and personal failure are normal and universal aspects of the human experience instead of feeling isolated in these struggles. When you make a mistake or face a setback, remembering that all humans struggle, fail, and experience pain helps normalize your experience and reduces the sense that you're uniquely flawed.

Mindfulness in self-compassion involves acknowledging your thoughts and feelings without being overwhelmed by them or pushing them away. This means recognizing when you're suffering without getting caught up in dramatic narratives about your pain. You can observe thoughts like "I feel terrible about this mistake" without automatically believing secondary thoughts like "This proves I'm worthless."

Building healthy self-worth also requires identifying and challenging the specific beliefs that undermine your sense of value. Cognitive behavioral therapy suggests that low self-esteem results from a complex cognitive process where negative self-beliefs, formed by negative life events, lead to the development of dysfunctional hypotheses that can engender maladaptive behaviors, resulting in a vicious circle. Common underlying beliefs include "I must be perfect to be worthy," "My worth depends on others' approval," or "Making mistakes proves I'm inadequate."

The process of identifying these beliefs often involves examining the "shoulds" and "musts" that govern your self-evaluation. Healthy self-worth involves replacing rigid standards with more flexible and realistic expectations. Instead of "I should never make mistakes," you might develop the belief "Making mistakes is part of learning and growing." Instead of "I must be liked by everyone," you might embrace "It's impossible and unnecessary for everyone to like me."

Developing competence in meaningful areas also contributes to healthy self-worth, but in a balanced way. Research indicates that high levels of intrinsic work values in adolescence—where work is meaningful, engaging, and a learning opportunity—are linked to positive emotions in adulthood. The key is pursuing competence for its own sake and for the positive impact it creates, rather than as a way to prove your worth or earn others' approval.

Self-compassion research reveals its practical benefits for building self-worth. Meta-analyses indicate that compassion-focused treatments are among the most powerful interventions for enhancing self-esteem, with cognitive behavioral therapy being particularly successful in promoting self-esteem in clinical and non-clinical populations. These interventions help people develop internal resources for maintaining self-worth even during challenging times.

Building healthy self-worth also involves learning to receive and internalize positive feedback while maintaining perspective about criticism. Many people with low self-worth dismiss compliments as undeserved or insincere while giving disproportionate weight to criticism. Developing a more balanced approach means taking in positive feedback without inflating your ego and considering criticism without devastation to your self-concept.

Another crucial aspect involves developing what researchers call "self-integrity"—maintaining your sense of worth even when facing threats to your identity or competence. Achieving self-integrity seems to require the elicitation of self-compassionate and self-protective strategies to process the internal monologue relating to various self-critics. This might involve reminding yourself of your values, past accomplishments, or growth areas when facing current challenges.

The practice of building healthy self-worth requires ongoing attention and maintenance. Self-esteem is a pervasive individual characteristic with major consequences for people's lives, demonstrating normative change and substantial individual differences in change across the lifespan. This means that self-worth naturally fluctuates based on life experiences, but the goal is to develop resilience and recovery strategies that help you return to a baseline of self-acceptance.

Regular self-compassion practices can help maintain healthy self-worth over time. While engaging in supportive self-talk, you might want to try gently stroking your arm, or holding your face tenderly in your hands. This physical self-comfort activates the parasympathetic nervous system and reinforces the emotional message of self-care. These practices help create new neural pathways that support self-acceptance and kindness rather than self-criticism and judgment.

Speaking Life Over Your Future

Speaking life over your future involves intentionally using language and visualization techniques that nurture hope, possibility, and positive expectations while remaining grounded in reality. This practice goes beyond mere positive thinking—it's about aligning your internal dialogue with your deepest values and highest aspirations, creating a mental environment where growth and healing can flourish. Cognitive reframing often includes journaling thoughts, engaging in self-reflection, and utilizing positive self-talk, with the goal of making positive thinking a more automatic response.

The power of future-focused language lies in its ability to shape not only your expectations but also your actions and decisions in the present moment. Brain imaging studies show that positive self-talk interventions modulate connectivity among motivation-related regions, while negative self-talk creates considerable alterations in self-referential, default mode, and reward-motivation networks. When you consistently speak about your future with hope and possibility, you're literally rewiring your brain to support the outcomes you desire.

Speaking life over your future begins with understanding the difference between healthy optimism and unrealistic fantasy. Healthy optimism acknowledges current challenges while maintaining confidence in your ability to grow, learn, and create positive change. It involves statements like "I'm learning to handle stress better" rather than "I'll never have problems again," or "I'm developing stronger relationships" rather than "Everyone will love me." This balanced approach maintains credibility with your subconscious mind while nurturing hope and motivation.

The practice involves consciously choosing language that implies growth, possibility, and forward movement. Instead of saying "I'm terrible at public speaking," you might say "I'm developing my public speaking skills." Rather than "I always mess up relationships," try "I'm learning to build healthier relationships." This shift from fixed identity statements to growth-oriented language creates space for change and improvement.

Visualization plays a crucial role in speaking life over your future. Research on the best possible selves intervention shows that expressing gratitude and visualizing positive futures can increase and sustain positive emotion. The "best possible self" exercise involves writing about yourself in the future, having achieved your goals and realized your potential. This isn't about creating unrealistic fantasies but about imagining a version of yourself that has grown through challenges and consistently applied positive changes.

The neurological impact of positive future visualization is significant. When you regularly imagine yourself succeeding, overcoming obstacles, and living according to your values, you activate the same neural networks that would be involved in actually achieving these outcomes. This mental rehearsal strengthens the neural pathways associated with confidence, problem-solving, and persistence, making positive behaviors more likely to occur naturally.

Time perspective plays a crucial role in speaking life over your future. Research shows that people with balanced time perspectives—who can learn from the past, engage with the present, and maintain hope for the future—tend to experience better mental health and life satisfaction. Speaking life over your future involves consciously expanding your time horizon beyond immediate difficulties to encompass long-term growth and possibility.

The language you use about your future should align with your core values and authentic aspirations rather than external expectations or societal pressures. Research shows that pursuing intrinsic values—where activities are meaningful, engaging, and provide learning opportunities—leads to more positive emotions and life satisfaction than pursuing extrinsic values focused solely on external validation. When your future-focused language reflects what truly matters to you, it carries more emotional power and motivation.

Affirmations can be part of speaking life over your future, but they must be credible and specific to be effective. Generic statements like "I am perfect" or "Everything always works out for me" may actually backfire if they conflict with your current experience. More effective affirmations focus on your capacity for growth and positive action: "I am capable of learning from my mistakes," "I have the strength to work through challenges," or "I am committed to treating myself with kindness."

The practice of speaking life over your future also involves reframing your relationship with setbacks and failures. Instead of viewing challenges as evidence that you're doomed to perpetual struggle, you can frame them as temporary obstacles that provide opportunities for growth and learning. Cognitive reframing helps people change how they feel, which may lead to altering their behavior. A person who feels less anxious about giving a work presentation might take on more responsibility and do better in the position.

Creating specific, values-based future narratives helps make your positive language more concrete and actionable. Rather than vague statements about "being happy," you might envision yourself "contributing meaningfully to my community through volunteer work" or "maintaining close relationships with family and friends." These specific images provide direction for your current choices and behaviors.

The concept of "implementation intentions" applies powerfully to speaking life over your future. These are if-then statements that connect specific situations with positive responses: "When I face a setback, then I will remind myself that this is temporary and I can learn from it." "When I feel discouraged, then I will recall three things I'm grateful for and one step I can take toward my goals." These pre-planned responses help maintain positive future focus even during difficult times.

Speaking life over your future requires consistency and patience. The process typically involves recognizing negative thought patterns, evaluating their validity, and developing alternative, more constructive views of specific situations. Just as negative thought patterns developed over time through repetition, positive patterns require consistent practice to become automatic. This doesn't mean forcing positivity during appropriate times of grief or processing—it means gradually shifting your default mental orientation toward hope and possibility.

The social dimension of speaking life over your future cannot be overlooked. Sharing your positive visions and goals with supportive friends, family members, or mentors can reinforce your commitment and provide external accountability. Research shows that people who articulate their goals and positive expectations to others are more likely to take action toward achieving them.

Regular practices can help maintain this positive future focus. Daily journaling about your hopes and aspirations, weekly visualization sessions, or monthly reviews of your progress toward meaningful goals all help keep your attention oriented toward possibility rather than limitation. Studies show that self-respect and positive self-talk alter brain states that are beneficial for potential performance improvement, suggesting that these practices have cumulative neurological benefits.

The ultimate goal of speaking life over your future is not to avoid all difficulties or guarantee specific outcomes, but to maintain hope, motivation, and resilience regardless of external circumstances. When you consistently frame your future in terms of growth, learning, and possibility, you create an internal environment that supports positive action and emotional wellbeing. This practice becomes particularly powerful during challenging times, when the tendency toward despair and hopelessness feels strongest.

Speaking life over your future represents a profound act of faith—not necessarily religious faith, but faith in your capacity for growth, in the possibility of positive change, and in the inherent worth of working toward something better. This faith, expressed through intentional language and visualization, becomes a powerful force for transformation that extends far beyond mere positive thinking into the realm of genuine life change.

CHAPTER 11: THE POWER OF GRATITUDE AND PRAISE

Jennifer had always considered herself a glass-half-empty person. It seemed natural to notice what was wrong, missing, or imperfect in any situation. When she received a promotion at work, her first thought was about the increased responsibilities and pressure. When friends complimented her appearance, she immediately focused on the flaws they must have missed. Her mental default setting seemed permanently tuned to a frequency that amplified problems while filtering out positives. She accepted this as simply part of her personality—until a conversation with her grandmother changed everything. "You know, dear," her grandmother said gently, "I used to be just like you. Spent forty years looking for what was wrong with everything. Then I learned something amazing: you can actually train your brain to see differently."

What Jennifer's grandmother intuitively understood, neuroscience has now proven with remarkable precision. Gratitude activates the brain's reward system, triggering the release of neurotransmitters such as dopamine and serotonin, commonly associated with feelings of pleasure and contentment. More extraordinary still, research has shown that regular gratitude practice can lead to lasting changes in the brain's structure and function, a phenomenon known as neuroplasticity. This isn't about forcing artificial positivity or pretending problems don't exist—it's about deliberately rewiring your neural pathways to naturally notice and appreciate the goodness that was always there but remained hidden by default patterns of thinking. This chapter will show you how to harness the scientifically-proven power of gratitude and praise to transform not only your own mental landscape but to create ripple effects of positivity that extend far beyond yourself. You'll discover specific, evidence-based practices that can literally change your brain's structure, improve your physical health, strengthen your relationships, and ultimately make gratitude and praise your default way of engaging with the world.

Rewiring Your Brain for Joy

The science of neuroplasticity reveals that your brain is not a fixed entity but rather a dynamic, changeable organ that reshapes itself based on your repeated thoughts and experiences. When we experience or express gratitude, our brains engage in a "gratitude circuit," a neural network activating regions involved in emotional processing, social bonding, and reward systems. This circuit includes the medial prefrontal cortex, essential for moral cognition and value judgments, and the hypothalamus, which regulates hormones responsible for critical functions like emotional responses and survival behaviors.

Understanding how gratitude rewires your brain begins with recognizing the specific neurochemical changes that occur during grateful thinking. When we express gratitude and receive the same, our brain releases dopamine and serotonin, the two crucial neurotransmitters responsible for our emotions, and they make us feel 'good'. Dopamine, particularly associated with feelings of reward and reinforcement, creates what researchers call a positive feedback loop. When expressing gratitude leads to feelings of happiness, you create a positive feedback loop: it gives you joy, and your brain uses dopamine to reinforce that link so that you repeat it.

The process of rewiring begins immediately but becomes permanent through consistent practice. By consciously practicing gratitude everyday, we can help these neural pathways to strengthen themselves and ultimately create a permanent grateful and positive nature within ourselves. This isn't wishful thinking—it's measurable brain change. A study in NeuroImage found that participants who kept a daily gratitude journal for three months showed increased gray matter in the prefrontal cortex. This structural change improves emotional regulation, decision-making, and sustained positivity.

One of the most remarkable aspects of gratitude's brain-rewiring effects is how it influences multiple neural networks simultaneously. Gratitude practices have been linked to decreased activity in the amygdala, the brain's fear center, leading to reduced stress and anxiety responses. When you regularly practice gratitude, you're not just feeling better in the moment—you're literally shrinking the brain structures associated with fear and stress while strengthening those connected to happiness and emotional regulation.

The reward processing system undergoes particularly significant changes through gratitude practice. Gratitude also enhances the brain's reward processing centers, including the nucleus accumbens, reinforcing a cycle of positive emotions. This creates what neuroscientists call an "upward spiral"—the more you practice gratitude, the more your brain becomes wired to notice things to be grateful for, which generates more gratitude, leading to further positive brain changes.

The social dimension of gratitude creates additional rewiring benefits. Expressing gratitude towards others stimulates the brain's release of oxytocin, prompting feelings of social connectedness. Oxytocin, often called the "bonding hormone," not only makes you feel more connected to others but also reduces cortisol levels and supports immune function. This means that practicing gratitude doesn't just make you feel more social—it actually improves your physical health while strengthening your neural capacity for forming meaningful relationships.

The prefrontal cortex, your brain's executive control center, experiences particularly beneficial changes through gratitude practice. Practicing gratitude also increases activity in the brain's prefrontal cortex, the area responsible for executive functions such as planning and emotional regulation. This enhanced prefrontal function helps explain why grateful people tend to make better decisions, show greater self-control, and experience less emotional reactivity to stressful situations.

Research on brain wave patterns reveals that gratitude practice induces measurable changes in electrical brain activity. Alpha waves are linked to a relaxed, meditative state that produces alpha waves. When the mind is experiencing gratitude, it produces more alpha waves, which are associated with calmness and relaxation. Additionally, gratitude and the associated ventral vagal state can produce gamma waves, which are linked to higher-level cognitive processing and a sense of calm connectedness.

The hypothalamus undergoes particularly important changes through gratitude practice, with wide-ranging effects throughout the body. Gratitude activates the hypothalamus as well, with downstream effects on metabolism, stress, and various behaviors.

Because the hypothalamus regulates hormones responsible for body temperature, emotional responses, appetite, and sleep, gratitude practice can improve virtually every aspect of your physiological functioning.

The timeline for neural rewiring through gratitude practice is both immediate and long-term. In studies, after eight weeks of practice, brain scans of individuals who practice gratitude have stronger brain structure for social cognition and empathy, as well as the part of the brain that processes reward. However, benefits begin much sooner—some studies show measurable brain changes within just a few weeks of consistent practice.

The neuroplasticity effects of gratitude extend beyond emotional centers to influence cognitive abilities. Regular gratitude practice enhances working memory, attention regulation, and cognitive flexibility. This occurs because gratitude actually changes your brain's neural pathways, combats chronic stress, and strengthens our immune system—generally boosting our well-being. The stress-reducing effects are particularly important because chronic stress actively damages neural connections, while gratitude helps repair and strengthen them.

One of the most exciting discoveries in gratitude neuroscience is how the practice influences the brain's attention system. UCLA neuroscientist Alex Korb explains that practicing gratitude alters the activity in your anterior cingulate cortex, enhancing your attention to positive aspects of your reality and increasing your ability to benefit from the good things in your life that are often overlooked. This means that gratitude practice literally trains your brain to notice positives that were always present but previously filtered out by negative attention biases.

The concept of "backward gratitude," "forward gratitude," and "final gratitude" represents sophisticated ways to leverage neuroplasticity for joy. "Backward gratitude" involves reminding yourself of achieved dreams, "forward gratitude" imagines that ten years from now, you'll look back at pictures of yourself and realize you looked pretty good, while "final gratitude" involves imagining activities as if they're the last time you'll do them. Each approach activates different neural networks, creating comprehensive brain rewiring for appreciation.

The autonomic nervous system also undergoes beneficial changes through gratitude practice. Research shows that our parasympathetic nervous system, or rest-and-digest, is triggered when we think about what we appreciate, versus focusing on the negative thought loop. This shift from sympathetic (stress) to parasympathetic (calm) nervous system activation helps maintain a healthy immune system, improves sleep quality, and supports optimal organ function.

Scientific Benefits of Thanksgiving

The research on gratitude's benefits has expanded exponentially in recent years, revealing effects that extend far beyond temporary mood improvements to encompass virtually every aspect of human health and wellbeing. Published July 2024 in JAMA Psychiatry, the new study drew on data from 49,275 women enrolled in the Nurses' Health Study, representing one of the largest longitudinal studies ever conducted on gratitude's health effects.

The mortality benefits of gratitude represent perhaps the most dramatic scientific finding. Participants with gratitude scores in the highest third at the study's start had a 9% lower risk of dying over the following four years than participants who scored in the bottom third. This reduction remained significant even after controlling for physical health, economic circumstances, and other aspects of mental health and wellbeing. Gratitude seemed to help protect participants from every cause of death studied—including cardiovascular disease.

The mental health benefits of gratitude practice have been documented across multiple systematic reviews and meta-analyses. Analysis of the results showed that patients who underwent gratitude interventions had fewer symptoms of depression with 6.89% lower score than that of the control group. Additionally, participants who underwent gratitude interventions had greater feelings of gratitude (up to 4% higher scores), greater satisfaction with life (6.86% higher), better mental health (5.8% higher), and fewer symptoms of anxiety and depression (7.76% and 6.89% lower scores, respectively).

The cardiovascular benefits of gratitude practice extend beyond mortality reduction to include measurable improvements in heart function. A 2021 review of research also finds that keeping a gratitude journal can cause a significant drop in diastolic blood pressure—the force your heart exerts between beats. The mechanisms behind these cardiovascular benefits involve the autonomic nervous system: taking a moment to be thankful causes physiological changes in your body that initiate the parasympathetic nervous system—the part of your nervous system that helps you rest and digest.

Sleep improvements represent another well-documented benefit of gratitude practice. Researchers from the University of Manchester in England examined the correlation between gratitude and the thoughts before sleeping, and how these affect an individual's sleep. The findings show that thinking positive thoughts before falling asleep promotes better sleep—and there's evidence that gratitude causes people to have positive thoughts about their life, social support and social situations.

Physical health improvements extend beyond cardiovascular and sleep benefits to include enhanced immune function and pain management. Practicing gratitude improves immune function, thus decreasing the risk of contracting diseases. Additionally, studies show that the daily practice of gratitude helps lessen an individual's sensitivity to pain. These effects occur because gratitude reduces chronic inflammation, which underlies many health problems.

The workplace benefits of gratitude have been extensively studied, revealing significant impacts on productivity and job satisfaction. A study conducted by Gallup shows that well-recognized employees are 45% less likely to leave after two years in a company. Moreover, The State of Recognition Report 2024 found the five traits of an effective employee recognition program: frequent meaningful recognition, flow-of-work integration, continual promotion, metrics that matter, and scalable personalized rewards.

A landmark study at the University of Pennsylvania demonstrates gratitude's immediate motivational effects. Researchers at the Wharton School randomly divided university fundraisers into two groups. One group made phone calls to solicit alumni donations in the same way they always had. The second group received a pep talk from the director of annual giving, who told the fundraisers she was grateful for their efforts. During the following week, the university employees who heard her message of gratitude made 50% more fundraising calls than those who did not.

The social and relationship benefits of gratitude practice have been documented across numerous studies. Gratitude has a social aspect to it that argues it to be a socially driven emotion. Social psychologists believe it to be entwined with the perception of what we have done for others and what others have done for us. Research shows that gratitude is an emotion that directly targets at building and sustaining social bondings and reinforce prosocial responses in the future.

Creative and cognitive benefits represent an often-overlooked aspect of gratitude's effects. Gratitude boosts dopamine production, which is associated with motivation and reward. This increase in positive brain chemistry enhances creative thinking and helps generate a larger number of ideas when tackling complex problems. The cognitive benefits extend to decision-making abilities, with gratitude enhancing decision-making skills through improved prefrontal cortex function.

Educational benefits of gratitude practice have been documented in multiple academic settings. When faced with challenges in education, gratitude helps foster resilience. For instance, acknowledging progress, no matter how small, sustains motivation while pursuing academic goals. This has proven particularly beneficial for non-traditional learners and those balancing studies with other responsibilities.

The stress-reduction benefits of gratitude involve multiple physiological mechanisms. Recent research has strengthened previous studies stating that journaling or writing about gratitude provides benefits to healthcare professionals, including physicians and registered nurses. These benefits include decreased stress and may contribute to a decrease in burnout among clinical and non-clinical healthcare workers. The stress reduction occurs through both psychological and physiological pathways, including reduced cortisol production and enhanced parasympathetic nervous system activation.

Resilience benefits of gratitude have been documented in populations facing various challenges. Gratitude can promote positive outcomes after a traumatic experience, which then helps establish resilience toward the adverse effects left by a negative encounter. This resilience enhancement occurs through gratitude's ability to facilitate meaning-making and positive reframing of difficult experiences.

The anti-inflammatory effects of gratitude practice represent an emerging area of research with significant health implications. Many benefits of gratitude also support heart health. Improving depression symptoms, sleep, diet and exercise reduces the risk of heart disease. These benefits occur partly through gratitude's ability to reduce chronic inflammation, which contributes to numerous health problems including cardiovascular disease, diabetes, and autoimmune conditions.

Interpersonal benefits extend beyond immediate relationships to include broader social impacts. Gratitude appears to have a domino effect. If a person experiences gratitude, they are more likely to recognize the help and then later reciprocate that help. This creates positive social cycles where people who are thanked are presumably more apt to extend help to others in the future.

Creating Daily Gratitude Practices

Establishing effective daily gratitude practices requires understanding both the science behind successful interventions and the practical realities of maintaining consistency over time. Meta-analyses and reviews have revealed that gratitude interventions often have mixed effects on gratitude or other health outcomes, making it crucial to implement practices that have been scientifically validated and personalized to individual needs and circumstances.

The foundation of effective gratitude practice lies in understanding the different types of interventions available. The gratitude interventions used in the studies varied between gratitude diaries, conversation programs, training, and visits, expression of gratitude to others (verbally or in writing), publishing pictures with captions of gratitude, and thinking of things that makes one feel grateful. Research shows that gratitude list was the most common strategy adopted, seen in eight of nine studies. This is known as the classic and basic gratitude intervention.

The gratitude journal represents the most studied and accessible daily practice. Two psychologists, Dr. Robert A. Emmons of the University of California, Davis, and Dr. Michael E. McCullough of the University of Miami, asked all participants to write a few sentences each week, focusing on particular topics. One group wrote about things they were grateful for that had occurred during the week. The results were remarkable: After 10 weeks, those who wrote about gratitude were more optimistic and felt better about their lives. Surprisingly, they also exercised more and had fewer visits to physicians than those who focused on sources of aggravation.

Frequency of practice significantly impacts effectiveness, with research revealing counterintuitive findings about optimal timing. Sonja Lyubomirsky and colleagues found that once or twice per week is more beneficial than daily journaling. This suggests that gratitude practice can become routine and lose its impact if overdone, making strategic timing important for sustained benefits.

The specificity of gratitude entries dramatically influences practice effectiveness. Rather than generic statements like "I'm grateful for my family," effective gratitude practice involves detailed, specific observations. For example, instead of writing "grateful for my partner," you might write "grateful that my partner noticed I was stressed about work and brought me tea without being asked." This specificity activates more neural networks and creates stronger emotional responses.

Behavioral expression of gratitude represents a powerful but underutilized practice. Behavioral gratitude expression was only included as part of a combined positive psychological program, there were no studies that incorporated behavioral gratitude expression only. However, research demonstrates significant benefits: Dr. Martin E.P. Seligman tested the impact of various positive psychology interventions. When their week's assignment was to write and personally deliver a letter of gratitude to someone who had never been properly thanked for his or her kindness, participants immediately exhibited a huge increase in happiness scores. This impact was greater than that from any other intervention, with benefits lasting for a month.

The three-good-things practice represents another scientifically validated approach that can be easily incorporated into daily routines. This practice involves writing down three things that went well during the day and explaining why you think each positive event occurred. Research shows this simple practice can increase happiness and decrease depressive symptoms for up to six months when practiced consistently.

Gratitude meditation combines mindfulness practices with appreciation, creating a powerful daily practice that can be done in just 5-10 minutes. This involves sitting quietly, bringing to mind something you're grateful for, and allowing yourself to fully experience the positive emotions associated with that gratitude. The key is to focus not just on the cognitive recognition of good things but on actually feeling the emotional experience of appreciation.

The gratitude visit represents an intensive practice that can create lasting positive changes. This involves identifying someone who has had a positive impact on your life, writing a detailed letter describing their impact and how it affected you, and then arranging to read the letter to them in person. While this practice requires more effort and courage than daily journaling, research shows it produces some of the strongest and most lasting increases in happiness and life satisfaction.

Photo gratitude practices leverage visual memory to enhance emotional impact. This involves taking photos of things you're grateful for or looking through existing photos while consciously cultivating gratitude for captured moments. The visual component activates additional neural pathways and can be particularly effective for people who are more visually oriented.

Morning and evening gratitude routines can bookend your day with positive experiences. A morning practice might involve identifying three things you're looking forward to and expressing gratitude for the opportunity to experience them. An evening practice could focus on three good things that happened during the day, regardless of how small they might seem.

Gratitude walks combine physical exercise with appreciation practice. During a 10-20 minute walk, you consciously notice things in your environment to appreciate—the warmth of sunlight, the color of flowers, the sound of birds, or the kindness of people you encounter. This practice combines the mood benefits of exercise with the neural benefits of gratitude.

Social gratitude practices extend appreciation beyond individual reflection to include others. This might involve sending one gratitude text message per day, expressing appreciation to coworkers, or sharing gratitude with family members during meals. This approach may be suitable even for busy workers because it is easy to understand and complete, without much time or special materials.

Micro-gratitude practices involve brief moments of appreciation throughout the day rather than dedicated practice sessions. This might include pausing to appreciate the taste of your morning coffee, feeling grateful for a comfortable chair, or appreciating a moment of quiet. These brief practices help train your brain to notice positives throughout the day rather than saving gratitude for designated times.

Gratitude challenges can provide structure and motivation for developing consistent practices. Popular approaches include 30-day gratitude challenges where you post daily gratitude on social media, or workplace gratitude challenges where teams share weekly appreciations. The social accountability component can enhance motivation and consistency.

Technology-assisted gratitude practices utilize apps and digital tools to support consistency and provide reminders. Many gratitude apps include prompts, reminders, and progress tracking features that can help maintain daily practices. However, research suggests that the medium is less important than the consistency and specificity of the practice.

Seasonal and holiday gratitude practices can provide natural rhythms for deeper appreciation work. Beyond traditional

Thanksgiving gratitude, you might create practices around birthdays (gratitude for growth over the past year), New Year's (gratitude for fresh starts), or personal milestones (gratitude for accomplishments and support received).

Troubleshooting common challenges in gratitude practice requires understanding typical obstacles and evidence-based solutions. Seventeen mental health professionals identified three contextual themes—cultural considerations, personal characteristics, and life experience—that were discussed as factors likely to influence intervention effectiveness. Understanding these factors helps personalize practices for maximum effectiveness and sustainability.

When Praise Becomes Your Default

The transformation of praise from an occasional practice to a default way of thinking represents a fundamental rewiring of your neural pathways and social patterns. When you practice gratitude—when you actively look for and acknowledge what your team members do well—you're rewiring your own brain for positivity. This neurological change creates what researchers call "positive attention bias," where your brain automatically scans for things worthy of appreciation rather than criticism.

Understanding the neuroscience of praise as a default reveals why this transformation is both possible and powerful. Giving recognition triggers the same dopamine release in managers that receiving it does for employees. When you acknowledge someone's good work, your brain rewards you for the prosocial behavior. This creates a reinforcing cycle where recognizing others literally makes you want to do it more. This means that the more you practice praise, the more naturally it comes to you.

The development of praise as a default occurs through what psychologists call "implementation intentions"—automatic if-then responses that become habituated through repetition. When praise becomes your default, you develop automatic responses like "When I notice someone doing something well, I immediately acknowledge it" or "When I see improvement, I automatically comment on it." These automatic responses require no conscious effort once established.

The distinction between effective and ineffective praise is crucial for developing sustainable default patterns. Behavior-specific praise that is contingent on the student's behavior alone is linked to positive outcomes for students, including enhanced academic engagement and reduced incidence of disruptive behavior. Generic praise like "good job" has minimal impact, while specific praise like "I noticed how you took time to help your colleague understand that concept—that showed real patience and care" creates lasting positive effects.

The 5:1 ratio represents a research-backed guideline for making praise your default in relationships and work environments. For maximum effectiveness, aim for at least 3 times more praise than discipline or corrective statements, with a ratio of 5 to 1 being ideal. This doesn't mean avoiding necessary feedback but rather ensuring that positive acknowledgment far outweighs criticism in your daily interactions.

Age-appropriate praise strategies help ensure that your default patterns are effective across different developmental stages. Positive feedback is the most effective for young children (8-9 years old), but negative feedback may be more effective for older children and adults (11-12 years old and up). Understanding these developmental differences helps you calibrate your default praise patterns for maximum impact.

The workplace implementation of praise as a default requires understanding organizational dynamics and individual preferences. Recognition for positive behavior strengthens the occurrence of similar responses in the future, making it a kind of positive reinforcement. In workplace settings, this might involve acknowledging effort rather than just results, recognizing collaboration and problem-solving, and highlighting character qualities like persistence and creativity.

Overcoming the cultural barriers to praise requires understanding societal patterns that discourage appreciation. Many cultures emphasize criticism and problem-solving over acknowledgment and appreciation, making praise feel unnatural or unnecessary. Some employers and employees are hesitant to engage in formal gratitude practices, often due to concerns about appearing unprofessional or insincere.

The authenticity of praise represents a critical factor in developing sustainable default patterns. Praise can improve children's intrinsic motivation and help them develop feelings of competence and better learning outcomes, but only when the praise is genuine and specific. Developing praise as a default means training yourself to notice genuinely praiseworthy actions rather than forcing artificial positivity.

Micro-praise practices help establish praise as a default through small, frequent acknowledgments. This might involve commenting on someone's good idea in a meeting, acknowledging a colleague's helpfulness, or appreciating a friend's listening skills. These brief moments of recognition compound over time to create significant relationship improvements and neural rewiring.

The timing of praise significantly affects its impact and your ability to make it a default. Reinforcers and punishments must happen at the time of the behavior to increase the likelihood of success. Immediate praise is far more effective than delayed recognition, which means developing the habit of expressing appreciation in the moment rather than saving it for later.

Social contagion effects multiply the impact when praise becomes your default. When a person witnesses how positive behaviors are recognized, such as praising a classmate's good academic grades as a result of his or her hard work, the adolescent as observer would imitate the positive behavior. This creates positive cycles where your default praise behavior influences others to adopt similar patterns.

The relationship between praise and identity formation makes this practice particularly powerful for children and adolescents. Positive behavior recognition is especially important to adolescent development because it promotes identity formation as well as cultivates moral reasoning and social perspective thinking from various social systems. When praise becomes your default with young people, you're helping shape their self-concept and values.

Self-praise represents an often-overlooked aspect of making praise your default. Many people who readily acknowledge others struggle to acknowledge their own efforts and accomplishments. Developing internal praise as a default means celebrating your own progress, effort, and growth with the same specificity and enthusiasm you show others.

The persistence of praise effects creates long-term benefits that justify the effort to make it your default. A study on the use of positive reinforcement in the classroom showed that it can be used to significantly improve students' age-appropriate behaviors and social skills, and the effects will last even after the reward system is removed or discontinued. This means that consistent praise creates lasting positive changes in others even when you're not present.

Environmental design can support the development of praise as a default through visual reminders and structured opportunities. This might involve keeping a journal of daily appreciations, setting phone reminders to acknowledge others, or creating team practices that build in regular recognition. The goal is to make praise easier to remember and implement until it becomes automatic.

The compound effects of praise as a default extend far beyond immediate interactions to create lasting cultural changes in families, teams, and organizations. Evidence indicates that this approach not only strengthens desirable behaviors but also enhances the quality of relationships between parents and children, and teachers and students. Over time, environments where praise is the default become more positive, productive, and emotionally supportive.

Personal barriers to praise often include fear of appearing weak, concerns about creating dependency, or beliefs that people should be intrinsically motivated without external recognition. Understanding these barriers helps you address them systematically. Research shows that current research supports praise's role in fostering moral development, reducing stress, and improving cognitive abilities like focus and working memory, providing evidence to counter these concerns.

The universality of praise needs means that making it your default serves a fundamental human requirement for recognition and validation. Such positive responses, rendered from various social systems, include tangible and intangible reinforcements. Everyone benefits from acknowledgment of their efforts and positive qualities, making praise a universally helpful default.

The integration of praise with constructive feedback represents advanced skill in making praise your default. This involves leading with acknowledgment of what's working before addressing what needs improvement, and ending feedback sessions with recognition of effort or character qualities. This approach maintains the positive neural environment that makes people receptive to growth while honoring their inherent worth.

Creating accountability systems helps ensure that praise becomes truly default rather than just occasional practice. This might involve asking trusted friends or colleagues to remind you when you're being overly critical, tracking your daily appreciations, or reflecting weekly on how well you're recognizing others. The goal is to make conscious what should become unconscious—a natural, automatic tendency to notice and acknowledge the good in people and situations around you.

CHAPTER 12: PROTECTING YOUR MENTAL ENVIRONMENT

David used to pride himself on staying informed. He read the news every morning, scrolled through social media feeds throughout the day, and participated in online discussions about current events. He considered himself educated and engaged, someone who cared about what was happening in the world. But lately, something had shifted. The constant stream of negative headlines, heated debates in comment sections, and endless notifications were taking a toll he hadn't anticipated. He found himself feeling anxious about things beyond his control, irritable with family members, and struggling to sleep at night as his mind replayed disturbing images and inflammatory arguments from his digital consumption. When his twelve-year-old daughter asked him why he seemed so angry all the time, David realized he had become a victim of his own mental environment—and he needed to learn how to protect it.

Your mental environment is just as real and influential as your physical environment, yet most people give little thought to what they allow into their psychological space. Just as you wouldn't knowingly drink contaminated water or breathe polluted air, you shouldn't passively consume toxic mental content without considering its impact on your emotional and cognitive well-being. Research reveals that the digital age has created unprecedented challenges for maintaining mental health, with problematic social media use among adolescents rising from 7% in 2018 to 11% in 2022, and studies showing direct correlations between excessive screen time and increased anxiety, depression, and sleep disturbances. This chapter will equip you with evidence-based strategies for guarding the gates of your mind, establishing healthy boundaries with media and relationships, and building a support system that nourishes rather than depletes your mental resources. The goal isn't to become isolated or uninformed, but to become intentional about curating an environment that supports your mental clarity, emotional stability, and overall psychological flourishing.

Guarding the Gates of Your Mind

The concept of guarding your mental gates originates from the understanding that your mind, like any complex system, can only process a finite amount of information before becoming overwhelmed or compromised. Research on cognitive load theory demonstrates that the human brain has limited capacity for processing information, and when this capacity is exceeded, decision-making quality, emotional regulation, and mental clarity all suffer. The gates of your mind represent the various entry points through which information, emotions, and influences can access your psychological space, including what you read, watch, listen to, and whom you interact with on a daily basis.

Understanding what constitutes the gates of your mind requires recognizing the multiple channels through which external influences shape your internal experience. Visual inputs include everything from social media feeds and news broadcasts to the books, movies, and advertisements you encounter. Auditory inputs encompass not only the music and podcasts you choose but also overheard conversations, background noise, and the general sound environment you inhabit. Social inputs involve the people you spend time with, their emotional states, communication patterns, and the values they express through word and action.

The neuroscience of mental gatekeeping reveals why this practice is crucial for psychological health. Digital media use and mental health research shows that constant connectivity can harm adolescents' mental health through multiple mechanisms, including sleep disruption, social comparison, cyberbullying exposure, and the displacement of face-to-face social interaction. When you fail to guard your mental gates, you subject your brain to what researchers call "continuous partial attention," a state where you're constantly monitoring multiple information streams without giving full focus to any single input.

Emotional contagion represents one of the most powerful phenomena that makes mental gatekeeping essential. Research demonstrates that emotions spread through social networks both online and offline, meaning that prolonged exposure to angry, anxious, or depressed individuals can literally change your own emotional state through unconscious mimicry and neural mirroring. This occurs because humans have evolved mirror neuron systems that automatically simulate the emotions and behaviors we observe in others, making emotional protection not just a luxury but a necessity for mental stability.

The challenge of mental gatekeeping in the digital age has been complicated by algorithms designed to capture and hold your attention regardless of the psychological cost. Social media platforms use sophisticated behavioral psychology to create what researchers call "persuasive design," employing variable ratio reinforcement schedules, social approval mechanisms, and fear-of-missing-out triggers to keep you engaged. These systems are explicitly designed to bypass your conscious filtering mechanisms, making intentional gatekeeping more important than ever.

Practical gatekeeping begins with awareness of your current mental inputs and their effects on your psychological state. This involves conducting what researchers call an "information audit"—systematically evaluating the sources of information and influence in your life and assessing their impact on your mood, energy levels, sleep quality, and overall well-being. You might track how you feel before and after consuming different types of media, noting patterns between specific inputs and changes in your mental state.

The timing of mental inputs significantly affects their psychological impact. Research on circadian rhythms and mental health shows that consuming stimulating or disturbing content close to bedtime can disrupt sleep quality, which in turn affects emotional regulation, cognitive function, and stress resilience the following day. Establishing "digital sunset" practices—cutting off stimulating media consumption 1-2 hours before sleep—represents a fundamental gatekeeping strategy that pays dividends across multiple aspects of mental health.

Curating your social media environment requires understanding that algorithms respond to your engagement patterns, meaning that what you like, share, comment on, and spend time viewing trains the system to show you more of the same. If you find yourself frequently engaging with negative, inflammatory, or anxiety-provoking content, you're inadvertently programming your feeds to deliver more psychological stress. Mindful engagement involves consciously choosing to interact with content that educates, inspires, or uplifts rather than content that triggers anger, fear, or comparison.

News consumption represents a particularly challenging area for mental gatekeeping because staying informed feels like a civic responsibility, yet research consistently shows that excessive news consumption, especially of negative or traumatic content, contributes to anxiety, depression, and a distorted perception of risk in the world. Effective news gatekeeping involves setting specific times for news consumption rather than allowing it to happen throughout the day, choosing quality sources over quantity, and balancing negative news with positive or solution-focused content.

The practice of mental gatekeeping extends beyond media consumption to include the conversations you engage in and the topics you allow to dominate your mental space. Research shows that repeatedly discussing negative events or engaging in what psychologists call "co-rumination"—dwelling on problems and negative emotions with others—can actually increase depression and anxiety rather than providing the emotional relief that people expect from venting.

Physical environment plays a crucial role in mental gatekeeping because your surroundings continuously send subtle messages to your subconscious mind. Cluttered, chaotic spaces can increase cortisol levels and make mental clarity more difficult, while organized, peaceful environments support cognitive function and emotional regulation. This extends to the visual content in your environment, including the images on your walls, the books on your shelves, and even the colors surrounding you.

Creating positive mental gates involves not just filtering out negative inputs but actively cultivating positive ones. This might include following accounts that share inspiring stories, beautiful imagery, or educational content; subscribing to podcasts that teach valuable skills or share uplifting perspectives; or joining communities focused on personal growth, creativity, or service to others. The goal is to bias your information diet toward content that nourishes your mind rather than depleting it.

The social aspect of gatekeeping requires recognizing that some relationships consistently drain your mental energy while others consistently restore it. Research on emotional labor shows that constantly managing other people's emotions or tolerating toxic behavior creates chronic stress that can lead to burnout and depression. Effective gatekeeping means setting boundaries with energy-draining relationships while investing more time and attention in relationships that support your growth and well-being.

Media, Relationships, and Mental Health

The relationship between media consumption and mental health has become one of the most significant psychological challenges of the 21st century, with research revealing complex interactions between digital engagement patterns and various aspects of psychological well-being. The pervasive influence of social media on daily life has sparked significant concern regarding its impact on mental health, with studies documenting correlations between excessive technology use and mental health issues including anxiety, depression, sleep disturbances, and attention difficulties.

Understanding the mechanisms by which media affects mental health reveals why mindful consumption is essential for psychological well-being. Social comparison theory explains one of the primary pathways through which social media can damage mental health—users frequently engage in upward comparisons, evaluating themselves against others who appear more successful, attractive, or happy, leading to negative self-evaluation and diminished self-worth. This phenomenon is amplified by the curated nature of social media content, where people typically share idealized versions of their lives rather than authentic representations of daily struggles and ordinary moments.

Research on digital media's impact on adolescent mental health reveals particularly concerning trends, with problematic social media behavior increasing significantly in recent years. More than 1 in 10 adolescents showed signs of problematic social media behavior, struggling to control their use and experiencing negative consequences. Girls reported higher levels of problematic social media use than boys (13% vs 9%), and over a third of young people reported constant contact with friends online, suggesting that digital connectivity has become a compulsive rather than intentional behavior for many.

The neurological impact of digital media consumption shows why these platforms can become psychologically addictive. Social media platforms trigger the release of dopamine through variable ratio reinforcement schedules—you never know when you'll receive a like, comment, or share, which creates the same neurochemical response pattern seen in gambling addiction. This explains why people often find themselves compulsively checking their devices even when they consciously want to reduce their usage.

Sleep disruption represents one of the most significant ways that media consumption affects mental health. The blue light emitted by screens can disrupt circadian rhythms by suppressing melatonin production, making it harder to fall asleep and reducing sleep quality. Additionally, the stimulating content consumed on devices—whether exciting, disturbing, or emotionally engaging—can keep the mind active when it should be winding down for rest. Research consistently shows that poor sleep quality is linked to increased anxiety, depression, irritability, and reduced cognitive function.

The phenomenon of "digital overwhelm" occurs when individuals consume more information than their cognitive systems can effectively process, leading to decision fatigue, reduced attention span, and emotional exhaustion. The average person encounters more information in a single day than previous generations encountered in weeks or months, creating constant pressure on mental resources that our brains have not evolved to handle effectively.

Cyberbullying and online harassment represent direct ways that digital relationships can damage mental health. Unlike traditional bullying, online harassment can be constant, anonymous, and widely visible, creating sustained psychological stress that can lead to depression, anxiety, and in extreme cases, self-harm or suicide. Research shows that victims of cyberbullying often experience symptoms similar to those of real-world trauma, including hypervigilance, avoidance behaviors, and intrusive thoughts.

The impact of media on body image and self-esteem has been extensively documented, particularly among young people. Constant exposure to filtered, edited, and curated images creates unrealistic beauty standards that can lead to body dissatisfaction, eating disorders, and low self-worth. The rise of influencer culture has intensified these effects by making idealized lifestyles and appearances seem both attainable and normal, when in reality they often represent carefully constructed fantasies supported by significant financial resources and professional teams.

Fear of missing out (FOMO) represents another pathway through which social media can negatively impact mental health. Constant exposure to other people's activities, achievements, and experiences can create anxiety about one's own life choices and a sense that everyone else is having more fun, success, or fulfillment. This can lead to compulsive social media checking, difficulty being present in one's own life, and chronic feelings of inadequacy or dissatisfaction.

The displacement effect of digital media consumption means that time spent online often replaces activities that are more beneficial for mental health, such as face-to-face social interaction, physical exercise, creative pursuits, or time in nature. Research shows that adolescents who spend more time in direct social interaction and less time on screens generally report better mental health outcomes, suggesting that the problem isn't just what digital media adds to our lives but also what it replaces.

However, research also documents potential benefits of digital media when used mindfully and intentionally. Online support communities can provide valuable emotional support and practical resources for individuals dealing with mental health challenges, chronic illnesses, or life transitions. Educational content can enhance knowledge and skills, while creative platforms can provide outlets for self-expression and connection with like-minded individuals.

The quality of online relationships can significantly impact their effect on mental health. Superficial interactions based on likes and comments tend to be less psychologically beneficial than deeper, more meaningful exchanges. Research shows that people who use social media primarily for direct communication with close friends and family experience more positive mental health outcomes than those who primarily consume content passively or engage in public posting for broader audiences.

Developing healthy relationships with media requires understanding the difference between active and passive consumption. Active consumption involves intentionally choosing specific content for particular purposes—learning a new skill, connecting with friends, or finding inspiration for a project. Passive consumption involves mindlessly scrolling through feeds, allowing algorithms to determine what you see, and using media as a default activity when bored or anxious.

The concept of "digital nutrition" provides a useful framework for understanding media consumption's impact on mental health. Just as junk food can provide immediate gratification while contributing to long-term health problems, "junk media"—content that is designed purely to capture attention without providing genuine value—can create short-term engagement while damaging long-term psychological well-being. A healthy media diet emphasizes high-quality content that educates, inspires, or genuinely entertains while limiting exposure to content that primarily triggers negative emotions or unhealthy comparisons.

Creating Healthy Boundaries

The establishment of healthy boundaries represents one of the most crucial skills for maintaining mental health and building satisfying relationships, yet many people struggle with boundary-setting due to cultural conditioning, fear of rejection, or lack of knowledge about what healthy boundaries look like in practice. Boundaries are the limits we set to protect our emotional, mental, and physical space, serving as guidelines for how we want to be treated and what behaviors are acceptable or unacceptable in our relationships.

Understanding the psychological foundation of boundaries begins with recognizing that they are essential for maintaining individual identity within relationships. Research shows that boundaries are driven by our view of our value as a person, and that healthy boundaries create healthy relationships while preventing enmeshment, codependency, and the loss of personal autonomy that can occur when individual limits are not clearly defined or maintained.

The mental health benefits of healthy boundaries are extensive and well-documented in psychological research. Setting clear boundaries reduces stress by minimizing the likelihood of being overwhelmed by others' demands or expectations, enhances relationships by leading to healthier and more respectful interactions, prevents burnout by helping individuals manage their energy and avoid overcommitting, and promotes independence by encouraging autonomy and empowering people to prioritize their own well-being.

Types of boundaries encompass multiple dimensions of human experience, each requiring different strategies and considerations. Physical boundaries protect your personal space and comfort levels, including preferences about touch, personal belongings, and physical proximity. Emotional boundaries protect your feelings and emotional energy, involving limits on how much emotional labor you provide to others and what kinds of emotional expression you're comfortable receiving. Mental boundaries protect your thoughts, values, and decision-making autonomy, including the right to hold different opinions and make choices without excessive input or pressure from others.

Temporal boundaries involve protecting your time and schedule from excessive demands or interruptions. With the rise of remote work and constant connectivity, maintaining clear boundaries around work hours, availability for communication, and time for rest and personal activities has become increasingly challenging yet essential for mental health. Research shows that blurred work-life boundaries are associated with increased stress, reduced job satisfaction, and poorer overall well-being.

Digital boundaries represent a modern necessity for mental health protection in an age of constant connectivity. These might include specific times when devices are turned off, limits on social media usage, guidelines for responding to messages and emails, and boundaries around sharing personal information online. Research demonstrates that people who maintain clear digital boundaries report better sleep quality, reduced anxiety, and improved face-to-face relationship satisfaction.

The process of identifying boundary needs begins with self-reflection and awareness of situations that consistently cause stress, resentment, or discomfort. These feelings often indicate areas where boundaries are needed but not currently in place. Common signs that boundaries are needed include feeling overwhelmed by others' demands, experiencing resentment in relationships, difficulty saying no to requests, feeling responsible for others' emotions or problems, and experiencing physical or emotional exhaustion in certain relationships or situations.

Communicating boundaries effectively requires clarity, consistency, and confidence, while also maintaining respect for others. Research shows that boundary-setting is most effective when it uses "I" statements to express needs without blaming or accusing others, provides specific rather than vague guidelines, and explains the reasoning behind boundaries when appropriate. For example, instead of saying "You always interrupt me," an effective boundary statement might be "I feel frustrated when I'm interrupted during conversations. I'd appreciate it if you would let me finish my thoughts before responding."

Common challenges in boundary-setting include fear of rejection or abandonment, guilt about prioritizing personal needs, cultural or family messages that discourage boundary-setting, lack of models for healthy boundaries in childhood, and fear of conflict or confrontation. Research shows that individuals who struggle with boundary-setting often have underlying beliefs about their worth being tied to their ability to meet others' needs, making boundary work closely connected to self-esteem and self-worth development.

Maintaining boundaries requires consistency and self-compassion, particularly when others test or push against newly established limits. Research indicates that boundaries often get tested more intensely when they're first implemented, as people who benefited from the absence of boundaries may resist the changes. This testing period requires persistence and the understanding that maintaining boundaries is an ongoing practice rather than a one-time conversation.

Workplace boundaries present unique challenges due to power dynamics, professional expectations, and economic pressures. Healthy workplace boundaries might include clear communication about working hours and availability, limits on after-hours communication, boundaries around personal information sharing, and guidelines for handling workplace conflict or inappropriate behavior. Research shows that employees who maintain healthy workplace boundaries report higher job satisfaction, better work-life balance, and reduced symptoms of burnout.

Family boundaries can be particularly challenging to establish and maintain due to long-standing relationship patterns, emotional dynamics, and cultural expectations about family loyalty and obligation. Healthy family boundaries might involve limits on topics of conversation, guidelines for visiting and communication frequency, boundaries around financial support or assistance, and protection of personal decisions from excessive family input or criticism.

The relationship between boundaries and self-care reveals why boundary-setting is fundamentally an act of self-respect and self-preservation rather than selfishness. Research demonstrates that individuals who maintain healthy boundaries are better able to care for others sustainably because they're not operating from a depleted state. This challenges cultural messages that equate boundary-setting with being mean, selfish, or uncaring.

Boundary flexibility represents an advanced skill that involves adapting boundaries based on circumstances while maintaining core limits that protect essential well-being. This might mean being more available during a family crisis while still maintaining limits that prevent complete self-neglect, or adjusting work boundaries during busy periods while ensuring that temporary changes don't become permanent erosions of personal time and space.

The role of boundaries in modeling healthy relationships extends beyond personal benefit to include the positive impact on children, friends, and colleagues who observe boundary-setting in action. Research shows that children who grow up with adults who model healthy boundaries are more likely to develop strong boundary-setting skills themselves, while adults who demonstrate respectful boundary-setting often inspire others to examine and improve their own relationship patterns.

Building a Life-Giving Support System

A life-giving support system represents far more than a collection of casual acquaintances or social contacts—it constitutes a carefully cultivated network of relationships that actively contribute to your mental health, personal growth, and overall well-being through emotional support, practical assistance, and positive influence. Research consistently demonstrates that individuals with strong social support networks are 50% more likely to have better mental health outcomes, while social support has been associated with improved mental health through multiple pathways including stress reduction, enhanced coping resources, and increased resilience during difficult times.

Understanding the components of an effective support system begins with recognizing that different relationships serve different functions in promoting mental health and well-being. Emotional support involves relationships that provide empathy, understanding, and validation during both positive and challenging experiences. Instrumental support includes practical assistance such as help with tasks, resources, or problem-solving. Informational support comes from relationships that provide guidance, advice, and useful knowledge. Social support involves relationships that provide a sense of belonging, acceptance, and connection to a larger community.

The quality of support relationships matters more than quantity, with research showing that having a few deep, meaningful connections is more beneficial for mental health than having many superficial relationships. Life-giving relationships are characterized by mutual respect, emotional safety, reciprocity, and genuine care for each other's well-being. These relationships enhance your sense of self-worth rather than diminishing it, provide encouragement for your goals and growth, and offer honest feedback delivered with kindness and constructive intent.

Research on social support and mental health reveals that the perceived availability of support is often more important than the actual support received. This means that knowing you have people you can count on when needed provides psychological benefits even when you're not actively receiving help. This sense of security and connection serves as a buffer against stress and contributes to overall emotional resilience.

The neuroscience of social connection shows why building strong support systems is essential for mental health. Human beings have evolved as fundamentally social creatures, with social connection activating reward centers in the brain and triggering the release of oxytocin, which reduces stress hormones and promotes feelings of well-being. Conversely, social isolation activates the same pain centers in the brain as physical injury, explaining why loneliness can be genuinely painful and why strong relationships are not a luxury but a necessity for psychological health.

Building a life-giving support system requires intentionality and effort, particularly in a culture that often prioritizes individual achievement over community building. The process begins with assessing your current relationships and identifying which ones consistently provide energy, encouragement, and positive influence versus those that drain energy, create stress, or undermine your well-being. This assessment helps you understand where to invest more time and energy and where you might need to create more distance or boundaries.

Diversifying your support system across different contexts and relationship types provides resilience and prevents over-dependence on any single relationship. A healthy support system might include family members who provide unconditional love and historical perspective, friends who share common interests and provide fun and companionship, mentors who offer guidance and wisdom based on experience, colleagues who understand professional challenges and provide career support, and community members who share values and provide opportunities for service and contribution.

The cultivation of support relationships requires the development of social skills including active listening, empathy, vulnerability, and the ability to both give and receive help gracefully. Research shows that people who are good at maintaining friendships tend to be generous with their time and attention, reliable in their commitments, and skilled at creating positive shared experiences. They also know how to be appropriately vulnerable, sharing their authentic selves while respecting boundaries and social norms.

Creating opportunities for connection requires stepping outside comfort zones and being proactive about building relationships. This might involve joining groups or organizations aligned with your interests or values, volunteering for causes you care about, attending community events or classes, participating in religious or spiritual communities, or simply being more intentional about deepening existing relationships through regular communication and shared activities.

The digital age presents both opportunities and challenges for building life-giving support systems. Online communities can provide valuable connections for people with shared interests, experiences, or challenges, particularly for those who may feel isolated in their immediate geographic communities. However, research shows that online relationships are most beneficial when they complement rather than replace face-to-face interactions, and when they involve meaningful exchange rather than passive consumption of others' content.

Maintaining support relationships requires ongoing investment and attention, particularly during busy or stressful periods when it might be tempting to withdraw from social connection. Research indicates that relationships require regular nurturing through communication, shared experiences, and mutual support. This might involve scheduling regular check-ins with important people in your life, remembering and acknowledging significant events in their lives, and being present and supportive during their challenges and celebrations.

The concept of "social fitness" suggests that building and maintaining relationships requires the same kind of intentional practice and attention as physical fitness. Just as physical fitness requires regular exercise, good nutrition, and rest, social fitness requires regular interaction, emotional nurturing, and attention to relationship health. This includes skills like conflict resolution, forgiveness, and the ability to navigate the natural ups and downs that occur in long-term relationships.

Reciprocity represents a crucial element of healthy support systems, involving the balance between giving and receiving help, attention, and care. Research shows that relationships where one person consistently gives while the other consistently takes become unsustainable and can lead to resentment, burnout, and eventual relationship breakdown. Healthy support relationships involve mutual investment, with both parties contributing to each other's well-being in ways that feel natural and sustainable.

The role of professional support within a comprehensive support system acknowledges that some needs are best met by trained professionals rather than friends and family. Therapists, counselors, coaches, medical professionals, and other specialists can provide expertise, objectivity, and specialized interventions that complement personal relationships. Recognizing when professional support is needed and being willing to seek it represents an important aspect of building a comprehensive support system.

Creating boundaries within support relationships ensures that helping others doesn't come at the expense of your own well-being. Research on caregiving and mental health shows that individuals who provide extensive support to others without maintaining their own boundaries and self-care are at risk for burnout, depression, and health problems. Sustainable support involves knowing your limits, communicating them clearly, and ensuring that your own needs are being met even as you care for others.

The long-term cultivation of a life-giving support system requires understanding that relationships evolve over time and that different seasons of life may require different types of support. Some relationships may become closer while others naturally drift apart, some support needs may increase while others decrease, and new relationships may need to be formed as circumstances change. Maintaining flexibility and openness to relationship changes while preserving core connections that consistently provide mutual benefit creates a dynamic and resilient support system that can adapt to life's inevitable transitions and challenges.

CHAPTER 13: THE DISCIPLINE OF MENTAL RENEWAL

The journey of transforming your thought life is not a destination you reach once and never have to revisit. Instead, it's an ongoing discipline that requires the same kind of intentional cultivation as tending a garden. Just as a gardener must consistently water, weed, and nurture their plants to see them flourish, the practice of mental renewal demands daily attention, purposeful habits, and a commitment to growth that extends far beyond moments of crisis or difficulty. The process of learning how your thoughts, feelings and behaviors interact helps you view challenging situations more clearly and respond to them in a more effective way through structured, goal-oriented approaches.

What makes this discipline both challenging and beautiful is that it transforms from a conscious effort into a natural way of being. Research shows that it takes an average of 66 days for a behavior to become automatic (a habit), but for some people it can take as long as 8 1/2 months. The thoughts that once required deliberate intervention to redirect gradually become patterns of wisdom and strength that flow naturally from a renewed mind. When you embrace mental renewal as a lifestyle rather than a quick fix, you're choosing to invest in a future version of yourself that approaches life's inevitable challenges with resilience, clarity, and an unshakeable foundation of truth. This chapter will equip you with the practical tools and biblical wisdom necessary to make thought management not just a temporary practice, but a transformative way of life.

Making Thought Management a Lifestyle

The transition from occasional thought management to a sustainable lifestyle begins with understanding that transformation happens through consistent, small actions rather than dramatic overhauls. Routines provide a sense of order and structure, reducing stress and uncertainty, while boosting efficiency by reducing decision-making and helping us stay focused on our priorities. When you establish thought management as a core component of your daily life, you're creating a framework that supports mental health even during seasons when you don't feel particularly motivated or strong.

The foundation of lifestyle change rests on what researchers call "identity-based habits." Rather than simply trying to think better thoughts, you begin to see yourself as someone who naturally guards their mind and chooses truth over deception. This shift in identity is profound because it moves you from white-knuckling through difficult moments to living from a place of authentic transformation. Scripture supports this concept beautifully: "Therefore, if anyone is in Christ, the new creation has come: The old has gone, the new is here!" (2 Corinthians 5:17). Your new identity in Christ provides the motivation and power for sustainable change.

Self-care means taking the time to do things that help you live well and improve both your physical health and mental health, which can help you manage stress, lower your risk of illness, and increase your energy. Creating a lifestyle of mental renewal requires you to view thought management as an essential form of self-care rather than another burden on your already full schedule. This perspective shift is crucial because it reframes the discipline from something you "have to do" to something you "get to do" for your wellbeing.

The process of lifestyle integration begins with identifying the natural rhythms and transitions in your day where thought management can be seamlessly woven into existing routines. Many people find success by anchoring new mental habits to established behaviors—a technique psychologists call "habit stacking." For example, you might choose to practice gratitude while drinking your morning coffee, or engage in thought-testing exercises during your commute. The predictable rhythms of a structured routine can help reduce our anxiety levels by limiting the need for constant decision-making, which conserves mental energy.

One of the most effective strategies for making thought management a lifestyle is developing what cognitive behavioral therapists call "metacognitive awareness"—essentially becoming aware of your awareness. Cognitive behavioral therapy involves taking a close look at your thoughts and emotions to understand how your thoughts affect your actions, helping you unlearn negative thoughts and behaviors and learn to adopt healthier thinking patterns. This means noticing when you're noticing your thoughts, recognizing patterns in your thinking, and developing the skill of observing your mental processes without immediately reacting to them.

The beauty of metacognitive awareness is that it creates space between stimulus and response, allowing you to choose your thoughts rather than being unconsciously driven by them. Throughout your day, you can develop the habit of periodically checking in with your mental state, asking questions like: "What am I thinking about right now?" "Is this thought helpful or harmful?" "Does this align with what I know to be true?" These brief mental check-ins become second nature over time and serve as gentle course corrections that keep your thought life aligned with your values and goals.

Research has found links between family routines and children's social skills and academic success, demonstrating that routines are valuable for families during times of crisis. Similarly, when you establish thought management as a family or household practice, you create an environment where healthy thinking patterns are modeled and reinforced by those closest to you. This might involve sharing gratitude practices at dinner, discussing challenges and how to reframe them positively, or simply being open about your own thought struggles and victories.

Environmental design plays a crucial role in supporting a lifestyle of mental renewal. Just as you might remove junk food from your kitchen to support healthy eating, you can structure your environment to promote healthy thinking. This might mean limiting exposure to negative news or social media, choosing books and podcasts that feed your mind with truth and encouragement, or placing visual reminders of key Bible verses or affirmations in spaces where you spend significant time.

Routines create structure and let us know how we are doing, serving as indications to people around us of our wellbeing while creating a positive level of stress that keeps us focused and may help avoid depression. The goal is not to create a rigid, inflexible schedule but rather to establish reliable touchpoints throughout your day where mental renewal naturally occurs.

Technology can be both a help and a hindrance in developing sustainable thought management practices. While excessive screen time and social media consumption can fuel negative thought patterns, thoughtfully chosen apps, podcasts, and digital tools can support your mental renewal journey. Consider using meditation apps for guided thought exercises, journaling apps for processing difficult emotions, or even simple reminder notifications that prompt you to pause and assess your current mental state.

The key to long-term success lies in viewing thought management not as a perfect practice but as a progressive one. There will be days when you forget to engage your mental renewal habits, moments when you catch yourself spiraling into negative thinking patterns, and seasons when maintaining these practices feels particularly challenging. Rather than abandoning your efforts during these times, approach them with curiosity and compassion, viewing them as opportunities to strengthen your commitment and refine your approach.

Celebrating small victories is essential for maintaining motivation in lifestyle change. Acknowledge when you successfully redirect a negative thought, when you choose gratitude over complaint, or when you respond to stress with biblical truth rather than fear. These moments of recognition reinforce the neural pathways associated with positive change and build momentum for continued growth.

As thought management becomes more natural and automatic, you'll notice that your baseline mental state begins to shift. Where you once might have defaulted to worry or negativity, you'll find yourself naturally choosing faith and optimism. This doesn't mean you become unrealistic or dismiss legitimate concerns, but rather that your first instinct becomes one of trust in God's goodness and sovereignty rather than fear and anxiety.

Daily Practices for Mental Health

The establishment of daily practices forms the backbone of sustained mental health and thought transformation. Research demonstrates that consistent daily habits like getting quality sleep, eating a healthy diet, and exercising can significantly improve mental well-being, with even 15 minutes of stress-reducing activities positively affecting mental health. Unlike sporadic bursts of self-improvement that often fade when motivation wanes, daily practices create a stable foundation that supports your mental health regardless of external circumstances or internal feelings.

The morning hours offer a particularly powerful opportunity for establishing mental health practices because they set the tone for the entire day. Studies show that social relationships have positive impacts on our physical and mental health by reducing the impact of stress and fostering a sense of meaning and purpose in life. Beginning your day with intentional thought practices creates momentum that carries forward into your interactions, decisions, and responses to challenges throughout the day.

A comprehensive morning practice might include several components, each serving a specific purpose in mental health maintenance. Scripture reading and meditation provide spiritual grounding and fill your mind with truth before the day's demands begin. Psalm 1:2-3 describes the blessing of those who meditate on

God's law day and night: "their delight is in the law of the Lord, and on his law they meditate day and night. That person is like a tree planted by streams of water, which yields its fruit in season and whose leaf does not wither—whatever they do prospers."

Mindfulness and present-moment awareness practices involve being fully present without judgment, which can reduce stress, boost confidence, and improve overall mental well-being. Gratitude journaling, even for just five minutes, has been shown to improve mood, increase life satisfaction, and build resilience against negative emotions. The practice involves writing down three to five specific things you're grateful for, focusing on the details and emotions associated with each item rather than simply listing them.

Physical movement, even light stretching or a brief walk, activates the body's production of endorphins and helps regulate stress hormones. Moving your body releases endorphins, the brain's "feel good" neurotransmitters, which improve mood and mental health while reducing stress hormones and putting you into a calmer state where you can make more grounded decisions. The combination of physical activity with fresh air and natural light provides additional mental health benefits, particularly for those who struggle with seasonal mood changes or spend significant time indoors.

Midday practices serve as crucial reset points that prevent the accumulation of stress and negative thinking throughout the day. Relaxation and mindfulness are just as important as any other activities on your to-do list, if not more important, and should be worked into daily routines through meditation, deep breathing, and yoga. A brief mindfulness exercise—even two minutes of focused breathing—can interrupt stress cycles and return your nervous system to a calm state.

The practice of "thought auditing" during midday breaks involves honestly assessing the quality and direction of your thoughts since morning. Ask yourself: "What themes have dominated my thinking today?" "Have I been focusing on problems or solutions?" "Am I operating from faith or fear?" This brief self-assessment allows for course correction before negative thought patterns become entrenched.

Mindfulness practice through meditation and other mindfulness activities provides the opportunity to observe thoughts without judgment or reaction while staying grounded in the present moment, which builds the ability to be more flexible and adapt. Scripture memory work fits naturally into midday practices, particularly verses that address common mental health challenges like anxiety, depression, or discouragement. Philippians 4:6-7 offers powerful truth for anxious moments: "Do not be anxious about anything, but in every situation, by prayer and petition, with thanksgiving, present your requests to God. And the peace of God, which transcends all understanding, will guard your hearts and your minds in Christ Jesus."

Evening practices focus on processing the day's experiences, releasing accumulated stress, and preparing the mind for restorative sleep. Regular sleep schedule with consistent bedtime and wake times makes it easier to fall asleep at night and wake up in the morning, and adequate sleep helps regulate mood, stay focused, utilize healthy coping skills, and decrease stress hormones. The practice of "daily recapping" involves reviewing the day with intentional focus on growth, gratitude, and grace rather than dwelling on mistakes or disappointments.

Forgiveness practices, both for yourself and others, are essential components of evening routines. Carrying unforgiveness into sleep creates mental and emotional tension that interferes with rest and recovery. The practice might involve a simple prayer releasing the day's frustrations to God, or writing briefly about conflicts or difficulties with a focus on finding peace and resolution.

All healthy routines should include eating a nutrition-rich diet, exercising, and getting enough sleep, but no two routines will be exactly the same and may not even be exactly the same every day. Flexibility in daily practices is crucial for long-term sustainability. Life's demands vary from day to day, and rigidly adhering to a perfect routine can create additional stress rather than promoting mental health. The goal is consistency in intention rather than perfection in execution.

Meal times provide natural opportunities for mental health practices that are often overlooked. Eating healthy, regular meals and staying hydrated with a balanced diet and plenty of water can improve energy and focus throughout the day. Practicing mindful eating—paying attention to flavors, textures, and the experience of nourishment—creates moments of present-moment awareness that interrupt anxious thinking patterns.

Expressing gratitude before meals, whether through prayer or simple acknowledgment, connects you to the abundance in your life and cultivates a spirit of thankfulness that counters negative thinking. Even rushed meals can include brief moments of appreciation for the food, the people sharing the meal, or the strength to continue the day's activities.

Weekly practices provide opportunities for deeper reflection and planning that support daily mental health habits. A weekly "mental health inventory" might involve reviewing which practices served you well during the past week, identifying patterns in your thinking or mood, and making adjustments to your routine based on what you learned about yourself.

Sabbath rest, whether observed on Sunday or another day that works for your schedule, offers profound mental health benefits through the intentional cessation of productivity and the celebration of God's provision. Primary routines like regular healthy diet, sleep, and personal hygiene should be prioritized over secondary routines including leisure and social activities to maintain an overall regular daily living that directly enables positive mental health. This practice counteracts the mental health dangers of constant busyness and achievement-oriented thinking.

Social connections play a vital role in daily mental health practices. Building healthy relationships with friends, family, and peers can provide an outlet for stress and anxiety and act as a support system. Scheduling regular contact with supportive friends or family members, even through brief text messages or phone calls, maintains the social connections that are essential for emotional wellbeing.

The practice of "cognitive restructuring" can be woven throughout daily activities, involving the conscious replacement of negative or unhelpful thoughts with more balanced, truthful alternatives. CBT teaches people to challenge negative thought patterns and change their responses to unsettling situations, and has proven effective for treating anxiety, depression, and other mental health conditions. This might involve carrying index cards with encouraging Bible verses or personal affirmations that can be reviewed during difficult moments.

Technology boundaries are increasingly important daily practices for mental health. Constantly consuming information about other people's lives may cause someone to compare themselves and promote feelings of low self-worth, which increases feelings of anxiety and depression. Establishing specific times for checking email and social media, creating phone-free zones during meals or before bedtime, and choosing uplifting content over negative or sensational media all contribute to better mental health outcomes.

Handling Setbacks and Relapses

Understanding the nature of setbacks and relapses is fundamental to maintaining long-term mental health progress. About 50% of people will experience a relapse after having one episode of depression and that percentage increases after each additional episode, but there are steps you can take to reduce the impact of a relapse or recurrence or even prevent them altogether. Rather than viewing these experiences as failures or signs of weakness, it's crucial to understand them as normal parts of the recovery and growth process that can provide valuable information about your mental health patterns and needs.

Setbacks are a normal part of progress, and how individuals deal with setbacks plays a major role in recovery. The key distinction between a temporary setback and a more serious relapse lies in both duration and severity. A setback might involve a few days of increased anxiety, negative thinking patterns, or difficulty maintaining your usual mental health practices. A relapse typically involves a more significant return of symptoms that substantially interferes with daily functioning and may require professional intervention.

Mental illness relapse can be influenced by factors including stress, hormonal changes, and disruptions to treatment, with early detection making a significant difference in preventing the progression of symptoms. Recognizing early warning signs is perhaps the most important skill in preventing setbacks from escalating into more serious relapses. Common warning signs include changes in sleep patterns, increased isolation from friends and family, difficulty concentrating, return of negative thought patterns that had previously been managed, and decreased interest in activities that usually bring joy or satisfaction.

The emotional response to setbacks often determines their ultimate impact on your mental health journey. Recovering individuals tend to see setbacks as failures because they are unusually hard on themselves, which can set up a vicious cycle where individuals see setbacks as confirming their negative view of themselves. When you encounter a setback, your inner dialogue might include thoughts like "I'm back where I started," "I'll never get better," or "All my progress was fake." These thoughts, while understandable, can actually intensify and prolong the setback.

Developing a "setback response plan" before you need it provides a clear path forward during times when your thinking may be clouded by difficult emotions. Creating a relapse prevention plan includes identifying triggers, developing healthy coping mechanisms, and building a support system with people who can provide encouragement and accountability. This plan should include specific, concrete steps you can take when you notice early warning signs, contact information for supportive friends or mental health professionals, and reminders of coping strategies that have worked for you in the past.

Your setback response plan might include immediate comfort measures like taking a warm bath, listening to calming music, or engaging in gentle physical movement. It should also include practices that help you regain perspective, such as reading encouraging Bible verses, reviewing past victories and growth, or engaging in prayer or meditation. Proverbs 24:16 offers profound encouragement for these moments: "For though the righteous fall seven times, they rise again, but the wicked stumble when calamity strikes."

Recovery is a lifelong process that often involves changes across multiple domains of a person's daily life, including physical, behavioral, inter- and intra-personal, psychological, and social spheres. Professional support plays a crucial role in managing setbacks effectively. Knowing when to reach out for help is a sign of wisdom rather than weakness. Consider contacting a mental health professional when setbacks last longer than a week, when they significantly interfere with your ability to work or maintain relationships, or when you experience thoughts of self-harm.

The process of "setback analysis" involves examining what factors contributed to the setback without falling into self-blame or shame. When faced with a setback, taking the time to analyze the triggers that led to the relapse is important, as identifying these triggers can help develop prevention strategies for the future. Common triggers include major life stressors, changes in routine, relationship conflicts, physical illness, hormonal changes, or stopping beneficial practices like exercise or meditation.

This analysis should be conducted with curiosity rather than judgment, asking questions like: "What circumstances preceded this setback?" "Were there any changes in my routine or environment?" "Did I skip any of my usual mental health practices?" "What was my stress level in the days leading up to this?" The goal is to gather information that can help you recognize and address similar situations in the future.

A relapse isn't a sign that the person is 'weak' or a 'failure'—it's just a continuation of old coping patterns that need to be replaced with new ones. Reframing setbacks as learning opportunities rather than failures requires intentional practice but dramatically changes their impact on your overall mental health journey. Each setback provides data about your vulnerabilities, stress responses, and the effectiveness of your current coping strategies.

Building resilience against future setbacks involves diversifying your coping strategies so that you're not overly dependent on any single approach. Evidence-based behavioral treatments delivered in various formats including individual therapy, group therapy, and couples therapy can address underlying issues related to mental health struggles and increase coping skills to prevent relapse. This might mean developing both active coping strategies (like exercise or problem-solving) and passive coping strategies (like rest or acceptance), both social coping strategies (like talking to friends) and solitary strategies (like journaling or prayer).

The role of self-compassion in handling setbacks cannot be overstated. Research shows that people who treat themselves with kindness during difficult times recover more quickly and completely than those who engage in self-criticism. Working on your mental health from a place of care rather than self-punishment can do a lot more to improve your mental health and overall outlook than criticism and negative self-talk. This means speaking to yourself during setbacks with the same kindness you would offer a good friend facing similar struggles.

Practical self-compassion during setbacks involves acknowledging your pain without minimizing it, reminding yourself that struggle is part of the human experience, and treating yourself with gentleness rather than harsh judgment. You might say to yourself, "This is a moment of suffering. Suffering is part of life. May I be kind to myself in this moment."

Learning what tends to trigger your symptoms and recognizing them early can often help to prevent symptoms from worsening, and

233

committing to ongoing effort is the best strategy for ensuring that you stay well. Maintaining perspective during setbacks involves remembering that your current experience, while difficult, is temporary and does not define your entire journey. Creating a "victory journal" that documents past successes, overcome challenges, and moments of growth provides concrete evidence of your resilience during times when you feel hopeless or defeated.

The spiritual dimension of handling setbacks includes recognizing that God's love and acceptance of you does not fluctuate based on your mental health status. Romans 8:38-39 provides powerful reassurance: "For I am convinced that neither death nor life, neither angels nor demons, neither the present nor the future, nor any powers, neither height nor depth, nor anything else in all creation, will be able to separate us from the love of God that is in Christ Jesus our Lord."

Recovery from setbacks often happens gradually rather than dramatically. Relapsing is not a life sentence, and it should not discourage you to keep working on your mental health, as they are very common and even expected, with recovery tending to have its bumps in the road. Setting realistic expectations for the recovery process helps prevent additional disappointment and shame when progress feels slow.

Growing Stronger Through Challenges

The concept of post-traumatic growth—the idea that people can emerge from difficult experiences stronger and more resilient than before—fundamentally challenges the assumption that challenges only cause damage. Resilience acts as a protective layer against the development of mental health conditions like PTSD, anxiety, and depression, with a greater ability to recover from trauma, stress, and anxious tendencies helping people overcome difficulties instead of feeling consumed by them. Rather than simply surviving life's difficulties, it's possible to use them as catalysts for developing deeper wisdom, stronger character, and greater compassion for others.

Mental resilience is the ability to bounce back from adversity, stressful events and misfortune by adapting positively to life's challenges, with evidence suggesting that resilience can positively impact mental health outcomes. This growth doesn't happen automatically or without intentional effort. It requires a deliberate choice to engage with difficulties in ways that promote learning and development rather than simply enduring them until they pass.

The foundation of growing stronger through challenges lies in developing what psychologists call a "growth mindset"—the belief that abilities, intelligence, and character can be developed through effort, learning, and persistence. Cultivating a "growth mindset" involves viewing challenges as opportunities to learn and grow, rather than viewing abilities as fixed, and believing in the potential for improvement through dedication and hard work. This perspective transforms challenges from threats to opportunities and setbacks from evidence of inadequacy to information about areas for development.

Those with a positive mindset continuously practice shifting their perspectives during hard times, switching from thoughts of giving up to thoughts that accept what is happening and understand that they can build something better from it. Developing this mindset requires recognizing that your initial emotional response to challenges is normal and valid, but that you have the power to choose how you interpret and respond to difficulties over time.

The process of meaning-making plays a crucial role in growing stronger through challenges. Research shows that cultivating a sense of meaning in your life can contribute more to positive mental health than pursuing happiness. When you can identify how a difficult experience has contributed to your growth, helped you develop new skills, deepened your empathy for others, or strengthened your faith, the challenge transforms from senseless suffering into purposeful development.

Biblical wisdom consistently presents challenges as opportunities for growth rather than simply obstacles to endure. James 1:2-4 offers this perspective: "Consider it pure joy, my brothers and sisters, whenever you face trials of many kinds, because you know that the testing of your faith produces perseverance. Let perseverance finish its work so that you may be mature and complete, not lacking anything." This doesn't mean that challenges are enjoyable in the moment, but that they can serve a valuable purpose in your overall development.

Building resilience involves developing emotional strength and stability to confront and manage difficult emotions effectively, while maintaining the capacity to acknowledge, process and regulate feelings such as fear, sadness or anger in a healthy manner. One of the primary ways challenges contribute to growth is by expanding your emotional capacity and coping skills. Each difficulty you navigate successfully adds to your confidence that you can handle future challenges, creating a positive feedback loop that builds resilience over time.

The development of coping skills through challenges is often subtle and gradual. You might not realize in the moment that you're learning to tolerate uncertainty, developing patience, or building problem-solving abilities. People who are resilient have the strength and adaptability to adjust their mindset and behaviors in response to change or setbacks, allowing them to pivot, problem-solve and find new ways to navigate challenges. Reflection practices help you recognize and celebrate these developing strengths.

Creating a "challenge growth inventory" involves regularly examining how difficulties have contributed to your development. Ask yourself questions like: "What strengths have I discovered in myself through this challenge?" "How has this experience changed my perspective on what's truly important?" "What would I tell someone else facing a similar situation based on what I've learned?" "How has my faith been deepened or refined through this difficulty?"

Building a social support network involves developing and maintaining a solid network of supportive relationships with friends, family, and other trusted individuals. Challenges often reveal the depth and quality of your relationships, sometimes surprising you with unexpected support while also clarifying which relationships truly sustain you during difficult times. This relational clarity, while sometimes painful, ultimately contributes to your emotional growth and helps you invest your energy in relationships that mutual nurture and encourage growth.

The capacity for empathy and compassion typically deepens through personal struggles. When you've experienced anxiety, depression, grief, or other challenges, you develop a unique ability to understand and support others facing similar difficulties. Resilience stems from the interaction of a person with their environment and the resulting processes that either promote well-being or protect them against the overwhelming influence of risk factors. This expanded capacity for compassion often becomes one of the most meaningful outcomes of working through personal challenges.

Spiritual growth frequently occurs during seasons of difficulty as faith is tested, refined, and deepened. Many people report that their relationship with God became more authentic and intimate through struggles than it had been during easier seasons. Challenges have a way of stripping away superficial faith and revealing what you truly believe about God's character, love, and sovereignty. Psalm 34:18 offers comfort during these refining seasons: "The Lord is close to the brokenhearted and saves those who are crushed in spirit."

Embracing the idea that setbacks are not failures, but rather opportunities to learn valuable lessons that can contribute to future success. The practice of "challenge reframing" involves consciously choosing to view difficulties through the lens of potential growth rather than simply surviving them. This doesn't mean denying the pain or difficulty of your circumstances, but rather asking how you can use the experience to become stronger, wiser, or more compassionate.

Practical steps for growing stronger through challenges include maintaining practices that support your mental health even when they feel difficult, seeking learning opportunities within struggles, connecting with others who have faced similar challenges, and regularly reflecting on your growth and development. Practicing self-care activities should promote physical, emotional, and mental wellbeing, including getting adequate sleep, eating a healthy diet, exercising regularly, and finding time for relaxation and hobbies.

The development of wisdom through challenges is often one of the most valuable outcomes of difficult experiences. Wisdom differs from knowledge in that it involves not just understanding information but knowing how to apply it wisely in various situations. Resilient individuals reflect on past experiences, extract valuable lessons and use setbacks as stepping stones toward greater resilience and wisdom. This wisdom becomes a gift you can offer to others facing similar struggles.

Creating legacy from your challenges involves consciously choosing to use your experiences to help others, whether through formal mentoring, sharing your story, volunteering with organizations that address issues you've faced, or simply being a supportive presence for friends and family members going through difficulties. This transformation of personal pain into service to others often provides profound meaning and purpose that helps integrate challenging experiences into your overall life story.

Most importantly, resilience can be learned, practiced, developed, and strengthened, with individuals potentially being more resilient at different times in their lives than others. The goal is not to become invulnerable to future challenges but to develop the confidence that you can grow through whatever life brings your way. This confidence comes not from believing that life will be easy, but from knowing that you have the resources, skills, and support necessary to handle difficulties constructively.

The ultimate growth through challenges involves developing what might be called "antifragility"—not just bouncing back to your previous state after difficulties, but actually becoming stronger and more capable because of them. Cultivating positive self-talk and treating yourself with compassion allows you to build more mental resilience when it comes to getting through future challenges. This represents the highest form of resilience and reflects the biblical promise that "all things work together for good for those who love God and are called according to his purpose" (Romans 8:28).

The discipline of mental renewal, when embraced as a lifestyle supported by daily practices and strengthened through the wise handling of setbacks and challenges, creates a foundation for mental health that can weather any storm. As you continue this journey, remember that transformation is not a destination but a process, and every step forward—even the small ones—contributes to the renewal of your mind and the strengthening of your faith.

CHAPTER 14: THINKING LIKE JESUS IN EVERY SITUATION

There comes a moment in every believer's journey when the question shifts from "What would Jesus do?" to "How would Jesus think?" This transformation represents a profound deepening of spiritual maturity—moving beyond external imitation to internal transformation. When Paul wrote that "we have the mind of Christ" (1 Corinthians 2:16), he wasn't speaking metaphorically or suggesting a distant aspiration. He was declaring a present reality available to every follower of Jesus who chooses to align their thinking patterns with divine truth.

The mind of Christ isn't simply accessed during moments of crisis or major decision-making; it becomes the lens through which we process every situation, relationship, and circumstance. Changing the way you think changes your perspective which changes how you act in the world, as Jesus challenged people to change their thinking because regardless how many times you read through the Bible, if your mind doesn't change, you will simply impose your biases and labels on the words you read. This chapter will explore how to develop Christ-centered perspectives that naturally flow from a transformed mind, moving from reactive patterns to responsive wisdom, operating from love as your mental foundation, and walking in the divine wisdom that comes from intimate relationship with God. The goal isn't perfection but progression—developing thought patterns that increasingly reflect the heart, character, and priorities of Jesus in every area of life.

Developing Christ-Centered Perspectives

The development of Christ-centered perspectives begins with understanding that Jesus didn't simply teach a new way of thinking—He embodied a completely different operating system for the human mind. The mind of Christ embraces Christ's exclusive claim and cares about pointing people to "the Way," with the understanding that Fed Ex doesn't drop off the "mind of Christ" on your doorstep the day you're saved. Where the world operates from scarcity, fear, and self-preservation, Jesus demonstrated abundance, faith, and sacrificial love. Where human nature defaults to judgment, comparison, and competition, Christ modeled grace, acceptance, and service.

Understanding the foundation of Christ-centered thinking requires recognizing that Jesus operated from a fundamentally different set of assumptions about reality than the world around Him. God's way of thinking is different to the pattern of the world, and when we meditate on the truth of verses about renewing our minds, we can overcome the influence of negative thoughts in our lives. He saw people not as they appeared but as they were created to be. He viewed circumstances not as random events but as opportunities for God's glory to be revealed. He understood suffering not as meaningless pain but as purposeful preparation for greater good.

The practical development of Christ-centered perspectives involves learning to ask different questions when faced with any situation. Instead of "How does this affect me?" we learn to ask "How might God use this for His glory and others' good?" Rather than "What do I deserve?" we consider "How can I serve?" Instead of "Why is this happening to me?" we explore "What might God be teaching me through this?" These perspective shifts don't happen overnight but develop through consistent practice and intentional submission to the Holy Spirit's guidance.

Scripture is our source for knowing what is true, honorable, just, pure, lovely, and commendable, and we have been given whole new minds in Christ where what we choose to think about as Christians matters. One of the most transformative practices for developing Christ-centered perspectives is regular meditation on Philippians 4:8: "Finally, brothers and sisters, whatever is true, whatever is noble, whatever is right, whatever is pure, whatever is lovely, whatever is admirable—if anything is excellent or praiseworthy—think about such things." This verse provides a filter for evaluating not just our thoughts but our perspectives on everything we encounter.

The "whatever is true" component challenges us to base our perspectives on biblical truth rather than cultural assumptions, personal feelings, or popular opinion. When facing financial difficulties, the truth might be that God promises to provide for our needs (Philippians 4:19), not that we're destined for poverty. When dealing with difficult relationships, the truth includes God's call to love even our enemies (Matthew 5:44), not permission to harbor bitterness or seek revenge.

"Whatever is noble" calls us to elevate our thinking beyond the mundane and temporary to focus on things of eternal significance. This doesn't mean ignoring practical concerns but rather approaching them from an elevated perspective that considers their role in God's larger purposes. A job loss becomes an opportunity to trust God's provision and possibly discover new directions. A health challenge becomes a chance to experience God's sustaining grace and deeper dependence on Him.

The practice of developing Christ-centered perspectives also involves learning to see people as Jesus sees them. Our brains are complex organs created by a loving God who never intended for us to absorb endless amounts of toxic messaging, as He fashioned our minds to be filled with all that is lovely and pure, noble and true. This means looking beyond surface behaviors to underlying needs, viewing annoying colleagues as image-bearers in need of grace, and seeing difficult family members as opportunities to practice unconditional love.

Christ-centered perspectives are particularly challenging to maintain during conflict or criticism. Jesus demonstrated this when religious leaders questioned His authority (Mark 11:27-33). Jesus refused to be pulled into playing their petty games, he did not allow them to bring him down to their level, and in a thoughtful response to their accusation, he pinned them against the wall—but in such a way that they couldn't even argue with him. Rather than reacting defensively or attacking their character, He responded with wisdom that both protected His mission and challenged their hearts.

The development of Christ-centered perspectives requires regular exposure to how Jesus thought and responded in various situations throughout the Gospels. This involves not just reading the red letters but studying the context, motivations, and principles behind Jesus' words and actions. When Jesus cleansed the temple, He wasn't acting in uncontrolled anger but responding to the perversion of His

Father's house with righteous indignation guided by love for true worship.

Environmental factors significantly influence perspective development. Instead of mindlessly scrolling social media, we mindfully study the Word of God; instead of fixating on the latest news headline, we fix our eyes on Jesus. This might mean limiting exposure to negative news that promotes fear and anxiety, choosing entertainment that elevates rather than degrades thinking, and surrounding yourself with people who encourage Christ-centered perspectives rather than worldly viewpoints.

Prayer plays a crucial role in developing Christ-centered perspectives because it aligns our hearts with God's heart and our minds with His thoughts. Regular prayer doesn't just present requests to God; it transforms our thinking by exposing us to His character, priorities, and ways of seeing situations. Through prayer, we begin to see challenges as opportunities for growth, difficulties as chances to experience God's faithfulness, and other people as precious to the heart of God.

The process of developing Christ-centered perspectives is ongoing and requires patience with yourself as you learn new patterns of thinking. It is a battle, and we are human, so it's okay to recognize when we aren't being governed by the Spirit and then take it captive immediately and surrender it at the feet of Jesus. Old perspective habits die hard, and there will be times when your first response to situations reflects worldly rather than Christ-centered thinking. The key is not perfection but progress—catching these moments more quickly and choosing to realign your perspective with biblical truth.

Accountability relationships can significantly accelerate the development of Christ-centered perspectives. When trusted friends or mentors can lovingly point out when our perspectives seem more aligned with worldly thinking than Christ's character, we gain valuable insight that might otherwise remain hidden. These relationships provide safe spaces to process difficult situations and receive wisdom about how to view them through the lens of faith rather than fear.

Responding vs. Reacting

The distinction between responding and reacting represents one of the most practical applications of developing the mind of Christ in daily life. Reacting is often impulsive, driven by emotional reactions in conflict, while responding is intentional and thoughtful, embodying effective communication strategies that de-escalate tension and build understanding. Understanding this difference and learning to implement responsive rather than reactive patterns can transform your relationships, reduce stress, and provide powerful testimony to the peace that comes from walking with God.

Reactions are essentially involuntary reflexes driven by emotions, past experiences, or unhealed wounds. A reaction is an involuntary, uncontrolled action resulting from external stimuli of some sort, much like when the doctor taps your knee with the mallet to test your reflexes. When someone criticizes us, our natural reaction might be to defend ourselves, criticize them in return, or withdraw in hurt. When circumstances don't go as planned, we might react with frustration, anxiety, or anger. These reactions are understandable and human, but they rarely lead to positive outcomes or reflect the character of Christ.

Responses, on the other hand, involve taking time to consider the situation, the people involved, and the desired outcome before choosing how to act. A response considers the situation, the feelings of everyone involved, and the ultimate goal of the conversation, seeking to de-escalate conflict, build understanding, and bring about a positive resolution. Responses require self-control and, more importantly, reliance on God's wisdom to guide our words and actions.

The biblical foundation for responsive rather than reactive living is found throughout Scripture. Proverbs 15:1 reminds us: "A gentle answer turns away wrath, but a harsh word stirs up anger," and Proverbs 29:11 says, "Fools give full vent to their rage, but the wise bring calm in the end." James 1:19 provides practical guidance: "My dear brothers and sisters, take note of this: Everyone should be quick to listen, slow to speak and slow to become angry." These verses outline a clear pattern of thoughtful response rather than immediate reaction.

Jesus modeled perfect responsive living throughout His earthly ministry. Jesus Christ experienced hatred, abuse, injustice, attacks of every sort, even severe beating and death—yet He never allowed Himself to just react. When Peter cut off the soldier's ear during His arrest, Jesus responded by healing the man and rebuking Peter's violence. When the crowd sought to make Him king by force, He withdrew to pray rather than being swept up in their enthusiasm. When religious leaders tried to trap Him with trick questions, He responded with wisdom that both answered their concerns and revealed their heart motivations.

The process of moving from reactive to responsive patterns begins with developing awareness of your emotional triggers and typical reaction patterns. Before responding, ask yourself why you're feeling triggered, and identify if the current conflict is tied to unresolved emotions or past experiences. Common triggers include feeling criticized, unheard, disrespected, or misunderstood. When you can identify what specifically triggers strong emotional reactions, you can prepare responsive strategies in advance.

Creating space between stimulus and response is crucial for developing responsive patterns. When emotions run high, take a moment to pause, as pausing gives you time to calm down, pray for wisdom, and consider your next words carefully—even a deep breath can create the space needed to move from reacting to responding. This pause might involve counting to ten, taking a deep breath, silently praying for wisdom, or even asking for time to think before responding to important conversations.

Prayer serves as the bridge between reactive impulses and responsive wisdom. Response is hitting a pause button and taking time to consider the situation, to pray, and to think about what is the right response in line with God's heart and purposes. In moments of potential reactivity, even a brief prayer like "Lord, give me wisdom" or "Help me respond like Jesus would" can provide the spiritual resource needed to choose a better path.

Active listening is a fundamental component of responsive interaction. Responding starts with truly listening to the other person, and James 1:19 encourages us to be quick to listen—when we listen to understand rather than to prepare our rebuttal, we're better equipped to respond with empathy and clarity. This involves setting aside your own agenda and defensiveness to truly hear not just the words being spoken but the emotions and needs behind them.

The practice of responsive living requires developing what might be called "emotional regulation skills." Responding biblically is not automatic; it takes a thorough understanding of scripture and an intentional effort to heed its instruction, involving listening well before speaking, seeking to understand the perspective and feelings of the other, and ultimately wanting to build up and restore rather than tear down and retaliate. This includes recognizing when your emotions are escalating and having predetermined strategies for managing them constructively.

Developing responsive patterns also involves challenging automatic thoughts that fuel reactive behaviors. When someone cuts you off in traffic, your automatic thought might be "They're so rude and inconsiderate!" A more responsive approach might consider "They might be dealing with an emergency" or "Everyone makes mistakes while driving." These alternative interpretations don't excuse poor behavior but prevent you from carrying anger and frustration that only hurts you.

The role of forgiveness cannot be overlooked in developing responsive rather than reactive patterns. The Bible teaches that we are never excused in doing wrong on the basis that we have been wronged, and our goal should be to learn to defer to and trust in Lord in matters of perceived attacks against us. Carrying unforgiveness creates emotional reactivity because unhealed wounds are easily triggered by present circumstances that remind us of past hurts.

Practicing responsive living in low-stakes situations builds the spiritual and emotional muscles needed for more challenging circumstances. This might involve choosing patience when stuck in traffic, responding kindly to a rude cashier, or listening without defensiveness when a family member offers unwanted advice. These everyday opportunities to choose response over reaction build patterns that serve you well in more significant conflicts.

Can you imagine the impact we would have in our workplace if, as Christians, we were responding more than reacting? Don't you think that to be truly conformed to the image of Jesus Christ, we need to ask God to help us become responders, to give us the grace and strength to get past our reactions and respond in a biblical way? The testimony of responsive living in our relationships, workplace, and community provides powerful witness to the transforming power of the Gospel.

Love as Your Mental Operating System

The concept of love as a mental operating system represents perhaps the most radical transformation available to the human mind. Love is the foundation for all that we do in the kingdom, and growing in love is foundational to our Kingdom assignment, with everything building upon God's love toward us. When love becomes the fundamental framework through which you process information, make decisions, and respond to people and circumstances, it creates an entirely different experience of life—one marked by peace, joy, and supernatural wisdom.

Understanding love as an operating system begins with recognizing that love, from a biblical perspective, is not primarily an emotion but a decision and a way of being. Love requires a conscious decision, a deliberate commitment to stand by someone through thick and thin, as seen in Deuteronomy 30:19-20 where we are called to choose life and love the Lord our God. While emotions certainly accompany love, basing your mental framework on love means choosing love-motivated thoughts and actions regardless of how you feel in any given moment.

The foundation of a love-based operating system is rooted in understanding God's love for you. Learning to receive God's love unconditionally brings healing to the wounds of the past and removes the shame and guilt that inhibits true God-given identity, with an antidote to negative thinking being to focus thoughts on all that is true, holy, just, pure, lovely, and worthy of praise. When you truly comprehend that you are unconditionally loved, accepted, and valued by the Creator of the universe, it transforms how you see yourself and others. You no longer need to operate from fear of rejection, scarcity, or the need to prove your worth.

Operating from love as your mental framework means filtering every thought, decision, and response through the question: "What is the most loving choice here?" This doesn't mean being permissive or avoiding difficult conversations, but rather approaching every situation with the goal of promoting genuine good for all involved. The Bible teaches that love and choose goodness go hand in hand,

and that we must actively choose to love others in a way that reflects the goodness of God. Sometimes love requires difficult conversations, setting boundaries, or refusing to enable destructive behaviors.

The practical implementation of love as a mental operating system begins with how you think about difficult people in your life. Instead of focusing on their flaws, mistakes, or how they've hurt you, a love-based operating system asks: "How can I see this person as God sees them?" "What might they need that could help them flourish?" "How can I contribute to their wellbeing while maintaining healthy boundaries?" This shift doesn't ignore real problems but approaches them from a foundation of goodwill rather than defensiveness or retaliation.

God's love gives a more accurate picture of who God is, helps us make wise decisions, and encourages belief in the sufficiency of the Word—when someone believes that God loves them and wants them to make decisions that honor Him, they trust that the Word will provide what they need to make such wise decisions. This understanding transforms decision-making from a fear-based process focused on avoiding negative outcomes to a love-based process focused on honoring God and serving others.

In practical terms, a love-based operating system changes how you approach everyday challenges. When facing financial pressure, instead of being consumed with worry about your security, you might focus on how God can use this situation to develop trust, teach you to rely on Him, or position you to help others facing similar challenges. When dealing with health issues, rather than being overwhelmed by fear, you can trust God's love and consider how your experience might enable you to comfort others or deepen your dependence on Him.

Love as an operating system also transforms how you process other people's words and actions. When someone speaks harshly to you, instead of immediately taking offense or planning retaliation, you might consider what pain or stress might be driving their behavior and how you can respond with grace. In 1 Corinthians 13:4-7, we find a blueprint for healthy love that emphasizes patience, kindness, compassion, and showing genuine care for the well-being of others. This passage provides specific guidance for how love thinks and acts in challenging situations.

The love-based operating system requires regular maintenance through practices that keep you connected to God's love and remind you of your identity as His beloved child. This might include daily meditation on verses about God's love, regular prayer focusing on thanksgiving for His faithfulness, and creating visual reminders of your belovedness that you can reference during difficult moments. In Christ, you are loved, accepted, and forgiven, and condemnation is both a work of our unrenewed mind and demonic powers—an unrenewed mind that does not know at a heart level they are loved will continually condemn oneself.

One of the most practical applications of love as an operating system involves how you talk to yourself. Some studies show we have about 3000 thoughts per hour or 50 per minute, and for many people, most of their thinking is negative, with some struggling with loving themselves and seeing themselves as God sees them. A love-based mental framework means speaking to yourself with the same kindness, patience, and encouragement you would offer a beloved friend. It means replacing self-criticism with truth about your identity in Christ and self-condemnation with reminders of God's grace.

The love-based operating system also influences how you approach goals and ambitions. Instead of being driven by the need to prove yourself, gain recognition, or achieve security, your motivation becomes serving God and others through your unique gifts and calling. This doesn't diminish excellence or effort but provides a healthier foundation that can sustain you through both success and failure.

Implementing love as your mental operating system requires patience with the learning process. Old patterns of fear-based, self-protective thinking don't disappear overnight. Love the Lord with all of your heart, mind, and soul as stated in Mark 12:30, and as negative thoughts come in, ask yourself, am I glorifying God right now in both your actions and your thoughts. The practice involves catching yourself when you're operating from fear, scarcity, or self-protection and consciously choosing to return to love-based thinking.

The ultimate fruit of operating from love as your mental framework is the peace that passes understanding described in Philippians 4:7. When your thoughts are rooted in God's love rather than fear, when your responses flow from love rather than defensiveness, and when your decisions are motivated by love rather than self-interest, you experience a stability and joy that circumstances cannot shake. This doesn't mean life becomes problem-free, but that you have a reliable foundation for navigating whatever comes your way.

Walking in Divine Wisdom

Walking in divine wisdom represents the culmination of Christ-centered thinking, moving beyond human understanding to accessing God's perspective and guidance for life's complexities. Wisdom is, first and foremost, from the Lord, and when you desire wisdom, be encouraged to go to him and his word in prayer, as the fear of the LORD is the beginning of wisdom. This wisdom doesn't simply provide better strategies for achieving human goals but reveals God's purposes and provides supernatural insight for living according to His will and ways.

Biblical wisdom differs fundamentally from worldly wisdom in its source, motivation, and outcomes. While earthly wisdom says always follow your heart, godly wisdom tells us in Jeremiah 17:9 that the heart is deceitful above all things; while earthly wisdom says seeing is believing, godly wisdom tells us in John 20:29 that blessed are those who have not seen and yet have believed. Divine wisdom acknowledges God as the source of all truth and aligns human thinking with His revealed character and principles.

The foundation of divine wisdom is the fear of the Lord, which doesn't mean being afraid of God but having a healthy reverence and respect for His character, authority, and ways. The reason that the fear of the Lord is the beginning of both knowledge and wisdom is that the moral life begins with reverence and humility before the Maker and Redeemer. This humble posture recognizes that God's ways are higher than our ways (Isaiah 55:9) and that our finite understanding needs His infinite perspective to navigate life wisely.

Accessing divine wisdom begins with recognizing the limitations of human reasoning and the need for God's guidance. Trust in the LORD with all your heart, and do not lean on your own understanding. In all your ways acknowledge him, and he will make straight your paths. This doesn't mean abandoning critical thinking but subordinating human reasoning to divine revelation and seeking God's perspective on important decisions and life directions.

Prayer serves as the primary channel for accessing divine wisdom. James addresses the believer who lacks wisdom in handling trials, stating that wisdom comes from prayer for God's help, as God gives generously with "single-minded" liberality and without reproach. This promise from James 1:5 assures believers that God desires to give wisdom to those who ask in faith, making prayer not just a religious duty but a practical necessity for wise living.

The study and meditation on Scripture provides the content and framework for divine wisdom. God desires to give His divine wisdom to His children, and all other types of learning are valuable but limited unless built upon the knowledge of the Lord Himself. God's Word doesn't just contain wise principles but reveals God's character, priorities, and ways of thinking that inform every aspect of life. Regular engagement with Scripture through reading, study, memorization, and meditation fills the mind with divine perspectives that shape decision-making and problem-solving.

Walking in divine wisdom requires developing discernment—the ability to distinguish between God's voice and other influences vying for your attention. Let no one deceive you with empty words, for because of these things the wrath of God comes upon the sons of disobedience, and believers should try to discern what is pleasing to the Lord. This discernment comes through growing familiarity with God's character as revealed in Scripture and increasing sensitivity to the Holy Spirit's guidance.

Divine wisdom often contradicts conventional wisdom and cultural expectations. Jesus demonstrated this when He taught that the greatest should be servants (Matthew 20:26), that losing your life leads to finding it (Matthew 16:25), and that loving your enemies represents the highest form of love (Matthew 5:44). Walking in divine wisdom means being willing to follow God's ways even when they seem counterintuitive or unpopular.

The practical application of divine wisdom involves bringing God into every decision-making process, not just major life choices. Wise decisions are decisions that bring God glory, and Jesus didn't live in a way as to avoid the cross, but He willingly chose it. This might mean seeking God's guidance about how to handle a difficult conversation with a coworker, how to respond to financial pressure, or how to prioritize your time and energy.

Developing divine wisdom also requires learning from the wisdom literature of Scripture, particularly Proverbs, Ecclesiastes, and Job. These books provide practical guidance for living wisely in various circumstances while acknowledging the complexity and mystery of life. Knowledge tends to focus on correct understanding of the world and oneself as creatures of the magnificent and loving God, while wisdom is the acquired skill of applying that knowledge rightly, or "skill in the art of godly living."

Community plays a vital role in walking in divine wisdom. Proverbs frequently emphasizes the value of wise counsel and the danger of isolation in decision-making. Seeking input from mature believers, especially when facing important decisions, provides additional perspective and helps guard against self-deception or blind spots. This frees us from fearing the circumstantial results of our decisions, as we seek to honor Him and trust that His love will bring the results that are best for us (good or hard).

Walking in divine wisdom requires patience with God's timing and methods. Human wisdom often seeks the quickest, most efficient solutions, while divine wisdom sometimes involves waiting, taking seemingly indirect paths, or accepting circumstances that don't immediately make sense. Joseph's experience being sold into slavery and imprisoned before becoming second in command in Egypt illustrates how God's wisdom often unfolds over time in ways that initially appear devastating.

The cultivation of divine wisdom is a lifelong process that deepens through experience, study, and relationship with God. Each situation that requires wisdom—whether navigating relationships, making career decisions, handling finances, or facing health challenges—becomes an opportunity to seek God's perspective and learn to trust His guidance more fully.

The ultimate goal of walking in divine wisdom isn't to become a perfect decision-maker but to develop such intimacy with God that your thoughts naturally align with His thoughts and your choices reflect His character and purposes. God's love helps us make wise decisions by giving a more accurate picture of who God is, encouraging belief in the sufficiency of the Word, and providing clarity about what brings God glory. This transformation happens gradually as you consistently choose to submit your thinking to God's wisdom and allow His truth to shape your perspective on every aspect of life.

As you continue developing the mind of Christ through Christ-centered perspectives, responsive rather than reactive patterns, love-based thinking, and divine wisdom, remember that this is a journey of transformation rather than a destination to reach. Each day provides new opportunities to choose God's ways of thinking over the world's patterns, and each choice builds momentum toward the renewed mind that Paul describes in Romans 12:2. The goal isn't perfection but progress—becoming more like Jesus in your thinking patterns until His perspectives become as natural as breathing.

CHAPTER 15: HELPING OTHERS TAME THEIR THOUGHTS

The journey of mental renewal was never intended to be a solitary pursuit. When Jesus commissioned His disciples to "go and make disciples of all nations" (Matthew 28:19), He was establishing a pattern of transformation that flows from one life to another. As you've learned to recognize destructive thought patterns, challenge negative thinking, and align your mind with biblical truth, you've not only experienced personal freedom—you've been equipped to guide others toward the same liberation. The very struggles you've overcome become bridges of understanding that can carry hope to those still trapped in mental and emotional turmoil.

The transition from receiving help to offering help represents a sacred calling that goes far beyond casual encouragement or well-meaning advice. Christian family counselors help family members identify their challenges through the perspective of Biblical truths rather than by the dictates of their hearts, and show them how to work together using Bible-based principles to overcome their obstacles in a supportive, nurturing way. When you help others tame their thoughts, you participate in God's redemptive work of healing broken minds and restoring hope to weary souls. This chapter will explore how to become an effective minister of mental health in your spheres of influence, support loved ones in their journey toward mental freedom, create healthy family thought patterns that protect and nurture the next generation, and build communities where mental wellness flourishes. The goal isn't to replace professional counseling but to create networks of support where biblical truth and genuine care combine to offer hope and healing to those who desperately need both.

Becoming a Minister of Mental Health

The calling to become a minister of mental health emerges naturally from your own healing journey and grows into a purposeful commitment to use your experience for others' benefit. AACC is committed to assisting Christian counselors, the entire "community of care," licensed professionals, pastors, and lay church members with little or no formal training. It is our intention to equip clinical, pastoral, and lay care-givers with biblical truth and psychosocial insights that minister to hurting persons and help them move to personal wholeness, interpersonal competence, mental stability, and spiritual maturity. This doesn't require a formal degree in counseling or psychology, though these can certainly enhance your ability to help others. Rather, it begins with recognizing that your struggles with negative thinking, anxiety, depression, or other mental health challenges have equipped you with unique understanding and compassion for others facing similar battles.

The foundation of effective mental health ministry lies in understanding that you're not called to be a professional therapist but rather a wounded healer who offers hope, biblical perspective, and practical support. Many faithful face a unique tension when dealing with mental health issues: balancing their trust in God with the reality of their emotional pain. Questions like, "Why would God allow me to feel this way?" or "Is my depression a sign of weak faith?" are common and often require both theological and emotional care to answer effectively. Your role is to walk alongside others, share what you've learned about the connection between thoughts and emotions, and point them toward both professional help when needed and the spiritual resources that have sustained you.

Developing credibility as a mental health minister begins with your own ongoing commitment to mental wellness and continued growth. People facing mental health struggles can quickly sense whether someone truly understands their experience or is simply offering platitudes from a position of perceived superiority. Your vulnerability about your own journey, combined with evidence of genuine healing and growth, creates the authentic connection necessary for meaningful ministry. This means being honest about your ongoing challenges while also sharing the hope and practical strategies that have made a difference in your life.

The practical skills needed for mental health ministry include active listening, empathetic responding, knowing your limitations, and understanding when to refer someone to professional help. Mental health counseling relies on empirical research and established psychological theories, emphasizing the importance of evidence-based practices. Mental health counselors will seek specific training on these evidence-based practices and may use a variety of interventions tailored to the individuals' preferences and ways of learning and growing. While you may not have formal training in these areas, you can develop competency through reading, attending workshops, and learning from mental health professionals in your community.

Active listening involves giving someone your full attention, reflecting back what you hear, and asking clarifying questions that help them process their thoughts and emotions. This skill requires setting aside your own agenda and the urge to immediately fix or solve someone's problems. Often, people struggling with mental health issues don't need immediate solutions as much as they need to feel heard, understood, and less alone in their struggle. Your presence and willingness to listen without judgment can provide significant comfort and hope.

Empathetic responding goes beyond sympathy to actually entering into someone's emotional experience and responding from a place of genuine understanding. This doesn't mean taking on their emotions as your own, but rather communicating that you understand how difficult their situation must be and that their feelings are valid and understandable given their circumstances. Phrases like "That sounds incredibly difficult" or "I can understand why you would feel that way" validate their experience without minimizing their pain or offering premature solutions.

Understanding your limitations is crucial for effective mental health ministry because it protects both you and the people you're trying to help. Biblical counseling places the Bible as the ultimate framework. Practitioners in this field believe that spiritual guidance and adherence to biblical principles are essential for addressing mental and emotional struggles. You are not qualified to diagnose mental health conditions, prescribe medications, or provide therapy for severe mental illness. Your role is to offer support, encouragement, biblical perspective, and practical help while recognizing when someone needs professional intervention.

Knowing when to refer someone to professional help requires developing an understanding of warning signs that indicate serious mental health concerns. These include thoughts of self-harm or suicide, substance abuse, symptoms that significantly interfere with daily functioning, or situations involving domestic violence or abuse. When you encounter these situations, your responsibility is to encourage the person to seek professional help immediately and to provide them with appropriate resources and support during the referral process.

Creating boundaries in mental health ministry protects both your own mental health and the effectiveness of your help to others. This includes setting limits on your availability, not becoming someone's only source of support, and maintaining appropriate emotional distance that allows you to care without becoming overwhelmed or codependent. Healthy boundaries actually enhance your ability to help others by ensuring that you remain emotionally and spiritually healthy enough to offer genuine support over time.

The spiritual dimension of mental health ministry involves recognizing that mental and emotional struggles often have spiritual components and that God's truth and presence provide essential resources for healing. Research shows that integrating spiritual dimensions into therapy can lead to increased gratitude, optimism, and overall mental well-being. Families engaging in this type of counseling often experience a deeper sense of spiritual fulfillment and connection with one another. This doesn't mean that all mental health issues are spiritual problems, but rather that addressing the spiritual dimension alongside emotional and practical concerns often provides the most comprehensive and lasting help.

Prayer plays a central role in mental health ministry, both as a resource you offer to others and as a practice that sustains your own ability to help. Praying with someone who is struggling can provide comfort, hope, and a tangible reminder of God's presence and care. However, prayer should complement rather than replace practical help and professional intervention when needed. Teaching others to pray about their thoughts and emotions, to bring their fears and anxieties to God, and to seek His guidance in their healing process provides them with resources that extend far beyond your direct involvement in their lives.

Scripture provides a foundational framework for understanding mental health from a biblical perspective and offers practical principles for mental and emotional healing. Jesus was an amazing listener, He helped people reflect on their choices, and He supported people in His community through their hardest times. What an amazing gift He was and continues to be to those who are in need mentally and spiritually. Sharing relevant Bible verses, helping others understand how biblical truth addresses their specific struggles, and teaching them to use Scripture as a resource for mental renewal becomes a key component of effective mental health ministry.

Building a network of resources enhances your ability to help others by ensuring that you can connect people with appropriate professional services, support groups, and additional resources that meet their specific needs. This might include relationships with Christian counselors, psychiatrists, support groups, online resources, and community mental health services. Having these connections established before you need them allows you to respond quickly and effectively when someone requires help beyond what you can provide.

Training opportunities can significantly enhance your effectiveness as a mental health minister. MHC provides research, resources, and services aimed at proactively improving mental health and wellbeing, especially for ministry leaders. Many organizations offer courses in crisis intervention, suicide prevention, grief counseling, and other topics relevant to mental health ministry. While these don't qualify you as a professional counselor, they can provide valuable skills and knowledge that improve your ability to help others safely and effectively.

Supporting Loved Ones in Their Journey

Supporting family members and close friends through mental health struggles requires a unique blend of love, patience, wisdom, and endurance that goes beyond general mental health ministry. Like many illnesses and diseases, mental health disorders tend to run in the family and can be passed down from parent to child. This risk increases even more if both parents have a mental health disorder. When someone you love deeply is battling depression, anxiety, trauma, or other mental health challenges, the stakes feel higher, the emotions run deeper, and the temptation to take on responsibility for their healing can become overwhelming. Learning to support loved ones effectively while maintaining healthy boundaries and realistic expectations is essential for both their recovery and your own well-being.

The foundation of supporting loved ones begins with understanding that you cannot fix or cure someone's mental health issues, but you can provide consistent love, encouragement, and practical support that creates an environment where healing becomes more possible. It's important to know just because a parent has a mental health condition doesn't necessarily mean it will have an impact on their children. This perspective shift from trying to solve their problems to walking alongside them in their journey relieves you of

266

impossible pressure while allowing you to focus on what you actually can control—your own responses, attitudes, and actions.

Educating yourself about your loved one's specific mental health challenges provides crucial context for understanding their behavior, emotions, and needs. Depression, anxiety, bipolar disorder, PTSD, and other conditions each have unique characteristics, symptoms, and treatment approaches. Reading reputable books, attending support groups for families, and consulting with mental health professionals can help you develop realistic expectations and effective strategies for support. This education also helps you distinguish between symptoms of their condition and choices they're making, which can reduce frustration and increase compassion.

Creating a supportive environment at home involves establishing routines, reducing stress, and providing stability that supports your loved one's mental health without enabling unhealthy behaviors. Positive family dynamics are characterized by mutuality (cohesion and warmth), flexibility, open communication, and supportive relationships. These characteristics give children a sense of security and belonging and allow them to build trust, self-esteem, and stress-coping skills. This might include maintaining consistent meal times, creating quiet spaces for rest and reflection, limiting exposure to stressful situations when possible, and establishing family practices that promote mental wellness.

Communication strategies become particularly important when supporting loved ones with mental health challenges because these conditions can significantly affect how people process information, regulate emotions, and respond to others. Be upfront with your children and talk to them about mental health. Explain what it is and how treatments exist. Use your words carefully and avoid labels. The word "sad" is softer on the ears than "depressed" just as much as "scared" or "fearful" is more digestible to a child than "anxiety." Speaking calmly and clearly, avoiding criticism or blame, expressing love and support regularly, and listening without trying to immediately solve problems all contribute to more effective communication.

Setting appropriate boundaries protects both you and your loved one from the unhealthy dynamics that can develop when mental health issues strain family relationships. Hebrews 12:1 says that in order to run our race well, we need to shake off the things that keep us from reaching our goal. Ordering our home with healthy boundaries for kids and adults helps us do that. This includes not accepting verbal abuse or manipulation even when it stems from mental health symptoms, maintaining your own self-care practices, and refusing to enable behaviors that prevent your loved one from taking responsibility for their recovery. Boundaries are not walls that separate you from your loved one but rather frameworks that allow love to flow safely and sustainably.

Encouraging professional help requires sensitivity, timing, and persistence because many people struggling with mental health issues resist seeking professional treatment due to stigma, fear, or the effects of their condition on their thinking. Don't feel selfish if you need to prioritize getting help over caring for your family. Without you at full strength, your family will struggle to get by even if you're physically present. Approaching this topic with love, providing specific information about available resources, offering to help with appointments or transportation, and continuing to express support even if they initially refuse can eventually lead to acceptance of professional help.

Supporting medication compliance when it's been prescribed requires understanding that mental health medications often take time to work, may have side effects, and require ongoing monitoring by medical professionals. Your role is not to make decisions about medications but to encourage consistency, help monitor effects and side effects, and provide emotional support during the adjustment process. Never encourage someone to stop taking prescribed medications without consulting their doctor, even if they seem to be feeling better.

Crisis intervention skills become essential when supporting loved ones with mental health issues because these conditions can sometimes lead to suicidal thoughts, severe symptoms, or dangerous behaviors. Situations that are typically considered ACEs include the following. Being a victim of violence, abuse or neglect at home... Knowing the warning signs of suicide, having crisis resources readily available, and understanding when to call emergency services can literally save lives. This also includes having a crisis plan that outlines specific steps to take when symptoms escalate and ensuring that other family members understand their roles in supporting safety during difficult times.

Self-care for family members becomes crucial because the stress of supporting someone with mental health challenges can take a significant toll on your own emotional, physical, and spiritual well-being. They also discovered people who struggled with coping, rumination and blame — either toward themselves or their parents — were more likely to deal with mental health problems. This includes maintaining your own support system, pursuing activities that bring you joy and renewal, seeking professional counseling for yourself when needed, and practicing spiritual disciplines that sustain your faith and hope during difficult seasons.

Hope and realistic expectations must be balanced carefully when supporting loved ones through mental health challenges. Recovery is often a long process with setbacks and struggles, and improvement may be gradual rather than dramatic. Maintaining hope while accepting the reality of your loved one's condition helps you provide sustained support without becoming discouraged or resentful. The journey of Biblical family counseling is a grace-filled, redemptive process. It encourages families to grow closer to each other and to God, who is seen as the ultimate healer. This perspective allows you to celebrate small victories while maintaining patience for the longer journey ahead.

Family therapy or counseling can provide professional guidance for navigating the complex dynamics that mental health issues create within families. Typically, all family members attend therapy together. Sessions take place in a safe, supportive, Christ-centered environment, and are conducted by a trained, unbiased, nonjudgmental family counselor. These services can help family members learn better communication skills, understand each other's perspectives, and develop strategies for supporting recovery while maintaining healthy relationships. Even if your loved one is resistant to individual therapy, they may be more willing to participate in family counseling.

Creating Healthy Family Thought Patterns

The family environment serves as the primary training ground where children learn to think about themselves, others, God, and life circumstances. With the increasing rate of mental health disorders among youth in the United States (U.S.) and the essential role of parents in children's development, many studies have investigated the relationship between parental factors and children's mental health. The thought patterns that develop within families become deeply ingrained neural pathways that children carry into adulthood, influencing their mental health, relationships, and overall well-being for decades to come. Creating intentionally healthy family thought patterns requires understanding how thoughts are transmitted across generations, implementing specific practices that promote mental wellness, and addressing generational patterns that may be contributing to mental and emotional struggles.

The transmission of thought patterns within families happens through both explicit teaching and implicit modeling. Children learn much of their behavior from their parents; they end up doing what their parents do, rather than what their parents say they should do. So parents need to live up to the standards that they expect their children to observe. Children absorb not only what parents say about life's challenges but also how parents think about and respond to stress, disappointment, conflict, and uncertainty. When parents consistently model negative thinking patterns, catastrophic interpretations of events, or unhealthy coping mechanisms, children internalize these approaches as normal and carry them forward into their own lives.

Authoritative parenting emerges from research as the most effective approach for promoting healthy mental and emotional development in children. Authoritative parenting fosters confidence, responsibility, and self-regulation in children. These children manage negative emotions more effectively, leading to improved social outcomes and emotional well-being. By encouraging independence, authoritative parents help their children understand that they can achieve goals on their own, resulting in higher self-esteem. This parenting style combines high levels of warmth and support with clear expectations and boundaries, creating an environment where children feel secure while learning to think independently and make wise decisions.

Establishing family values that promote mental health requires intentional conversation and consistent reinforcement about what your family believes regarding emotions, challenges, relationships, and God's character. God points us toward seven virtues — traits of moral behavior — that will help our families avoid the habit of making destructive decisions. These traits, found in the free 7 Traits of Effective Parenting Assessment, are tangible and practical tools to help children mature into responsible adults. These values might include beliefs that emotions are valid and can be discussed openly, that asking for help is a sign of strength rather than weakness, that mistakes are opportunities for learning rather than reasons for shame, and that God's love remains constant regardless of circumstances.

Daily practices that reinforce healthy thinking include family gratitude sharing, where each member shares something they're thankful for each day, regular family devotions that emphasize God's faithfulness and love, and creating space for children to express emotions without fear of judgment or immediate correction. Mental health connects with every other component of our health, including our emotional, relational, physical, and spiritual health. Each of these has a profound impact on the other. If one is out of balance, our children's mental health can tip off-center. These practices don't need to be elaborate or time-consuming but should be consistent and age-appropriate.

Teaching children to identify and challenge negative thoughts provides them with lifelong skills for mental health management. This involves helping them recognize when they're engaging in all-or-nothing thinking, catastrophizing, mind reading, or other cognitive distortions, and then guiding them through the process of testing these thoughts against reality and biblical truth. That's why your children need a regular dose of "vitamin O" (optimism). Optimism is not about wishful thinking or hiding your head in the sand when things around you are challenging. Optimism is about holding on to the hope that something good can come from our circumstances, even when the situation looks grim. For younger children, this might involve simple questions like "Is that thought helpful or hurtful?" while older children can learn more sophisticated techniques for cognitive restructuring.

Modeling emotional regulation demonstrates to children how to manage difficult emotions in healthy ways rather than being overwhelmed or reactive. If children detect dissatisfaction and frustration about not having more money and material possessions, they will also feel worthless and inferior if they don't have them — that is simply the way our human nature functions. This includes showing children how to pause when feeling angry, take deep breaths when anxious, seek support when sad, and use spiritual resources like prayer and Scripture when feeling overwhelmed.

Children learn more from watching how parents handle emotions than from any verbal instruction about emotional management.

Creating safety for emotional expression requires establishing family norms that allow children to share their thoughts and feelings without fear of criticism, minimization, or immediate problem-solving. Alternatively, authoritative parenting is widely accepted to be the most healthy method of development for children. Authoritative parents are warm and nurturing yet also set clear limits and expectations. This means listening to children's concerns with empathy, validating their emotions even when you disagree with their interpretations, and helping them process difficult feelings rather than rushing to make them feel better or differently.

Addressing generational patterns involves recognizing unhealthy thought patterns or emotional responses that have been passed down through family lines and making intentional decisions to break these cycles. Single mothers have been found twice as likely to come from families where a parent had a mental health problem. This might include patterns of anxiety, depression, negative thinking, conflict resolution, or responses to stress that have characterized your family for generations. Breaking these patterns requires honest self-assessment, often professional help, and sustained commitment to developing new ways of thinking and responding.

Family meetings provide structured opportunities to address challenges, celebrate successes, and reinforce healthy thinking patterns. The counselor will also cover topics such as your spiritual beliefs and practices, whether or not you pray together, and how you have made it through tough times in the past. These meetings can include reviewing family values, discussing how everyone is doing emotionally, addressing conflicts or concerns, and planning family activities that promote mental wellness. The key is creating a format that feels supportive rather than punitive and gives every family member a voice in family decisions.

Technology boundaries become increasingly important for protecting family mental health in our digital age. There is questionable content at every turn in books, movies, and music. Questionable morals and ethics abound. Practices that the Bible stands against are becoming the norm. This includes establishing guidelines about screen time, social media use, and the types of content that are appropriate for different family members. It also involves modeling healthy technology use and creating tech-free times for family connection and conversation.

Professional support for families can provide valuable guidance for establishing and maintaining healthy thought patterns, especially when families are dealing with mental health challenges, trauma, or significant stress. Counselors guide families to view their challenges through the lens of biblical truths, which can provide a supportive and nurturing environment. This approach helps family members work together and tackle issues collaboratively. Family therapy, parenting classes, and mental health education can equip parents with tools and strategies that strengthen the family's ability to promote mental wellness for all members.

Building Communities of Mental Wellness

Creating communities where mental wellness flourishes requires intentional effort to build environments where people feel safe to share their struggles, receive practical support, and find hope for healing. How can a church become a sanctuary—a place where individuals living with mental health challenges feel safe, supported, and a sense of belonging? The Sanctuary Course was created to inspire and equip communities of faith that are asking this important question. Whether within churches, neighborhoods, schools, or other community settings, building mental wellness communities involves reducing stigma, providing education and resources, creating support systems, and fostering environments where both prevention and healing can occur.

The foundation of mentally healthy communities begins with leadership that prioritizes mental wellness and models vulnerability about mental health struggles. For too long, mental health struggles have been a quiet burden hidden in the shadows of many faith communities. While stigma surrounding depression, anxiety, trauma has decreased some in the past few years, other psychological challenges and pervasive mental illnesses have kept countless individuals from seeking help, even as they wrestle with these issues in the pews. When pastors, teachers, community leaders, and other influential figures share their own experiences with mental health challenges and demonstrate healthy ways of addressing them, it creates permission for others to be honest about their struggles and seek help when needed.

Education initiatives help communities understand mental health from both scientific and biblical perspectives, reducing misconceptions and fear that often prevent people from seeking help. This e-book provides a summary of the latest research findings from LifeWay Research on mental health and the church— along with helpful articles, brief medical overviews for acute mental illness, and recommended resources. This education might include workshops on recognizing signs of mental health issues, understanding the relationship between faith and mental health, learning basic crisis intervention skills, and exploring how communities can provide effective support without overstepping appropriate boundaries.

Support group development provides ongoing, peer-based support for people dealing with various mental health challenges while also educating family members and friends about how to provide effective support. Most have a connection to their local NAMI affiliate, but the groups are not necessarily sponsored by their affiliate. Some groups are sponsored by or meet in a church; one sprung up in a Community Mental Health Center. These groups might focus on specific conditions like depression, anxiety, or grief, or they might address broader themes like stress management, healthy relationships, or spiritual growth. The key is creating environments where people feel safe to share honestly without fear of judgment or unwanted advice.

Resource networks connect community members with professional mental health services, crisis intervention resources, and ongoing support services. Colorado Community Church also partners with many Christian mental health professionals who offer counseling in different areas of expertise. These counselors have been screened and vetted by CCC, and offer therapy from a Biblical worldview. Building these networks requires developing relationships with local mental health professionals, understanding what services are available and how to access them, and creating systems for connecting people with appropriate resources quickly when needs arise.

Crisis response systems ensure that communities can respond effectively when mental health crises occur, providing immediate support and connecting people with professional help. Contact Mental Health Professionals: Ask mental health professionals, therapists, or school counselors who can provide information about respected facilities that integrate spiritual approaches or offer Biblical counseling services as part of their programs. This includes training community members in suicide prevention, developing protocols for responding to mental health emergencies, and ensuring that professional crisis resources are readily available and accessible to community members.

Prevention programs focus on building resilience and mental wellness before problems develop, particularly targeting children, teenagers, and families facing risk factors for mental health challenges. Fearless is a strengths-based collective group experience designed to help young people pursue mental, emotional, social, and spiritual wellness. These programs might include stress management workshops, parenting classes that promote children's mental health, life skills training for teenagers, and community events that strengthen social connections and reduce isolation.

Integration with existing community structures leverages the relationships and resources that already exist within churches, schools, neighborhood organizations, and other community groups. Mental wellness is a lifelong process and a proactive strategy to strengthen our mental, emotional, social, and psychological resources. Rather than creating entirely separate mental health ministries, effective communities weave mental wellness into existing programs, ensuring that mental health considerations are integrated into youth programs, adult education, pastoral care, and community service initiatives.

Training and equipping community members provides the skills and knowledge necessary for creating sustainable mental wellness communities. The workbooks (group experience) are a Christ-centered and whole-person (whole-health) mental health approach that combines Scripture and practical tools to help individuals, couples, and families achieve mental well-being and healthy lives. This training might include Mental Health First Aid certification, crisis intervention training, grief support training, and ongoing education about mental health topics relevant to the community's needs.

Sustainability planning ensures that mental wellness initiatives continue over time rather than fading when initial enthusiasm wanes or key leaders move on. Create and sustain a leading network of trained Flourishing in Ministry coaches that support and equip ministry leaders for flourishing ministry. Train students for the sake of increasing mental health preparedness in the local church. This requires developing multiple leaders, securing ongoing funding or support, creating systems and procedures that can be maintained over time, and regularly evaluating and improving programs based on community feedback and changing needs.

Outreach efforts extend mental wellness support beyond the immediate community to reach people who might not otherwise have access to these resources. Churches that prioritize mental health support are better positioned to meet the needs of their congregations and local communities, becoming places of healing for those who might otherwise feel overlooked. This might include partnering with schools to provide mental health education, offering free community workshops on stress management or parenting, and creating online resources that can reach people beyond the immediate geographic area.

Evaluation and continuous improvement ensure that mental wellness communities remain effective and responsive to changing needs over time. This involves regularly gathering feedback from community members, tracking outcomes and impact, staying current with best practices in community mental health, and making adjustments to programs and approaches based on what is learned through experience. So if we are wanting to implement and integrate good mental health within the Church we need to not only do good mental health awareness at church and offer Christian resources for support for people with mental illness, but also to implement wellness and prevention resources. The goal is creating communities that not only address mental health problems when they arise but actively promote mental wellness and resilience for all community members.

The ultimate vision of communities of mental wellness is places where people experience the hope, healing, and transformation that God intends for every aspect of human life. Within our 2024 Annual Report, you'll read stories of people impacted through the work Sanctuary does in equipping the Church to support mental health and wellbeing—people like Cal, Suzie, Josh and many others. When communities successfully integrate biblical truth with practical mental health support, they become powerful witnesses to God's love and grace while providing tangible help to people who desperately need both spiritual and emotional healing. These communities reflect God's heart for wholeness and demonstrate that the church can be a place where mental health struggles are met with compassion, understanding, and effective support rather than judgment, stigma, or neglect.

As you step into the role of helping others tame their thoughts, remember that you're participating in God's redemptive work of healing and restoration. Whether you're supporting a family member through depression, creating healthier thought patterns in your home, or helping build a community where mental wellness flourishes, your efforts matter deeply to both God and the people whose lives you touch. The transformation you've experienced in your own thought life becomes a gift you can offer to others, multiplying hope and healing in ways that extend far beyond what you can see or imagine.

CHAPTER 16: YOUR NEW MIND, YOUR NEW LIFE

The transformation you've experienced throughout this journey represents far more than temporary relief from negative thoughts or a brief respite from mental struggles. What you've discovered is nothing less than the renewed mind that Paul described in Romans 12:2—a fundamental rewiring of your thought patterns that creates the foundation for an entirely new way of living. The Lord is the One who renews the mind and restores the soul, and God has given His children "a spirit not of fear but of power and love and self-control." This renewed mind doesn't simply think differently about problems; it operates from a completely different paradigm that sees challenges as opportunities, setbacks as setups for comebacks, and struggles as stepping stones to greater intimacy with God.

As you stand at this crossroads between your old patterns of thinking and the new life that stretches before you, it's important to pause and recognize the magnitude of what has occurred. You are no longer the same person who began this journey. The thoughts that once tormented you no longer have the same power. The lies that once seemed so convincing now sound foreign to your renewed mind. The fears that once paralyzed you have been replaced by faith that moves mountains. This chapter will help you celebrate the transformation that has already taken place, establish practices that maintain your mental health for the long term, continue growing and evolving in your journey, and step boldly into your identity as an overcomer who lives victoriously regardless of circumstances. Your new mind has created the possibility for a completely new life—one marked by freedom, joy, and the unshakeable peace that comes from knowing who you are in Christ.

Celebrating Your Transformation

The human tendency toward forward focus, while beneficial for progress, can sometimes rob us of the profound joy and encouragement that comes from acknowledging how far we've traveled. Biblical narratives and teachings offer timeless wisdom and comfort for those facing mental and emotional problems, and several biblical figures have faced emotional and psychological struggles, offering timeless lessons of faith and resilience. Celebrating your transformation isn't self-congratulation or prideful boasting; it's a spiritual discipline that honors God's faithfulness, strengthens your faith for future challenges, and provides testimony that can encourage others who are still struggling with the very issues you've overcome.

The practice of remembrance holds sacred significance throughout Scripture as God repeatedly called His people to remember His mighty works, establish memorials, and tell the stories of His faithfulness to future generations. When you take time to reflect on the specific ways your thinking has changed, the destructive patterns you've broken, and the new freedoms you've discovered, you're participating in this biblical tradition of remembrance. This isn't simply nostalgia or positive thinking; it's a spiritual practice that builds faith, increases gratitude, and provides concrete evidence of God's transforming power in your life.

Document the specific changes you've experienced by creating a detailed inventory of your transformation. Write down the negative thought patterns that once dominated your mind and contrast them with the truth-based thinking that now characterizes your mental life. Record the specific fears, anxieties, or depressive thoughts that used to control your decisions and emotions, then note how you now respond to similar situations with faith, peace, and biblical perspective. This documentation serves multiple purposes: it provides encouragement during future struggles, offers concrete evidence of God's faithfulness, and creates testimony that can bring hope to others facing similar battles.

Consider the relationships that have been restored or improved because of your mental renewal. Emotional and physical cravings for drugs or alcohol may continue for quite a while in recovery. Temptations to use again due to specific triggers, like people, places, or activities, can derail your hard-earned sobriety. When your thinking patterns changed, it likely affected how you interact with family members, respond to conflict, handle stress, and communicate with others. Healthy thinking creates the foundation for healthy relationships because you're no longer responding from places of insecurity, fear, or unhealed wounds but from confidence in your identity in Christ.

Acknowledge the dreams and goals that have become possible because of your transformed thinking. Mental health struggles often shrink our vision for the future, making us believe that survival is the best we can hope for rather than thriving. With renewed thinking comes renewed hope, expanded vision, and the courage to pursue purposes and callings that seemed impossible when your mind was trapped in negative patterns. Whether these goals involve career changes, ministry opportunities, creative pursuits, or relationship improvements, recognizing how mental renewal has opened new possibilities provides powerful motivation for continued growth.

Recognize the increased emotional capacity you now possess for handling life's inevitable challenges. The testing of faith produces endurance and maturity, and mental health struggles, while they are difficult, are not pointless. Before your transformation, difficult circumstances might have triggered automatic spirals into despair, anxiety, or hopelessness. Now you have tools for processing challenges, spiritual resources for finding peace during storms, and cognitive skills for maintaining perspective during temporary setbacks. This increased emotional resilience represents one of the most practical benefits of mental renewal.

The physical benefits of mental transformation often surprise people who expected only emotional or spiritual changes. Chronic stress, anxiety, and negative thinking patterns place tremendous strain on the body, contributing to sleep problems, digestive issues, headaches, muscle tension, and even compromised immune function. Self-care, both physical and spiritual, is a necessity. God is near to the brokenhearted and saves the crushed in spirit. As your thinking has become healthier, you may have noticed improvements in sleep quality, energy levels, physical tension, and overall health.

Celebrate the spiritual growth that has accompanied your mental renewal. The health of our thoughts is intimately connected to our spiritual vitality, and as you've learned to align your thinking with biblical truth, your relationship with God has likely deepened significantly. You may find that prayer feels more natural, Scripture reading is more meaningful, worship is more authentic, and your sense of God's presence is more constant. This spiritual growth often represents the most precious aspect of mental transformation.

Share your testimony with others who are struggling with similar issues, recognizing that your transformation story provides hope and encouragement to people who desperately need both. We have Jesus' example of taking breaks from the busyness of life to focus on spiritual matters, and He called His disciples to do the same. Your willingness to be vulnerable about your journey and honest about the changes you've experienced creates bridges of hope for others who may feel trapped in their current mental state.

Create rituals or traditions that mark your transformation anniversary, providing regular opportunities to remember God's faithfulness and celebrate your progress. This might involve annual retreats, special meals with family or friends who supported your journey, journaling exercises that compare your current state to previous years, or acts of service that honor God's goodness in your life. These celebrations serve as spiritual markers that remind you of how far you've come and encourage you during seasons when progress feels slow.

The celebration of your transformation isn't a one-time event but an ongoing practice that provides fuel for continued growth and motivation for persevering through future challenges. Mental health has gained much attention and acknowledgement in recent years, and from struggles with depression to battles with anxiety, there are Bible verses for mental health and Bible verses for mental illness that can help bring us peace. When you regularly acknowledge and celebrate the changes God has made in your thought life, you strengthen your faith, increase your gratitude, and build momentum for whatever transformations lie ahead.

Maintaining Long-Term Mental Health

The maintenance of mental health operates much like physical fitness—it requires consistent practices, ongoing attention, and adaptations as life circumstances change. There are always choices to make, some that can prove deleterious to recovery goals and even jeopardize sobriety entirely, while others, though difficult to accept and complete, are necessary to maintain forward momentum and progress in recovery. Long-term mental wellness isn't achieved through a single breakthrough or life-changing moment but through the daily decisions to implement healthy thought patterns, maintain spiritual disciplines, and respond to challenges with wisdom rather than reacting from old patterns of fear or negativity.

The foundation of sustainable mental health lies in understanding that mental wellness is a lifelong process and a proactive strategy to strengthen our mental, emotional, social, and psychological resources rather than a destination you reach and can then ignore. Just as physical health requires ongoing attention to diet, exercise, and medical care, mental health requires consistent practices that nourish your mind, strengthen your emotional resilience, and deepen your spiritual roots. This perspective helps you approach mental health maintenance with realistic expectations and sustainable practices rather than perfectionist standards that set you up for discouragement.

Daily spiritual disciplines provide the non-negotiable foundation for long-term mental health because they keep your mind aligned with biblical truth and your heart connected to the source of all healing. This includes consistent time in prayer, regular Scripture reading and meditation, worship that focuses your thoughts on God's character and goodness, and gratitude practices that counteract the human tendency toward complaint and negativity. When our mental health is compromised, we often feel alone and isolated, but these disciplines remind us that we are never alone—even when we are dealing with trials and tribulations.

Cognitive maintenance involves the ongoing practice of monitoring your thoughts, challenging negative patterns when they arise, and consciously choosing truth-based thinking over emotion-driven reactions. This doesn't mean you become hyper-vigilant about every thought but rather that you develop the habit of periodic mental check-ins that assess the quality and direction of your thinking. Any thought entertained long enough stands a good chance of becoming an action. And any action repeated over time has the potential of becoming a habit. When you notice patterns of worry, negativity, or fear beginning to develop, you have tools for interrupting these patterns before they gain momentum.

Physical health practices significantly impact mental wellness because the mind and body are interconnected systems that influence each other constantly. Regular exercise releases endorphins that improve mood, reduce stress hormones, and provide natural anxiety relief. Adequate sleep allows your brain to process emotions, consolidate memories, and restore chemical balance. Proper nutrition provides the building blocks for neurotransmitter production and stable blood sugar that affects mood and cognitive function. He gives strength to the weary and increases the power of the weak, and maintaining physical health provides a stable foundation for mental wellness.

Emotional regulation skills require ongoing practice and refinement as you encounter new stressors, life transitions, and unexpected challenges. This includes developing healthy ways to process and express emotions, building tolerance for uncomfortable feelings without immediately trying to escape or numb them, and learning to respond rather than react when emotions run high. The goal isn't to eliminate difficult emotions but to experience them without being controlled by them and to use them as information about your needs, values, and circumstances.

Relationship maintenance plays a crucial role in long-term mental health because isolation and unhealthy relationships can quickly undermine even the strongest mental wellness practices. This involves nurturing relationships with people who support your mental health journey, setting appropriate boundaries with those who don't, and developing skills for healthy communication and conflict resolution. Support systems provide accountability, encouragement, and practical help during challenging seasons, making them essential infrastructure for sustained mental wellness.

Stress management becomes increasingly important as life brings new responsibilities, challenges, and transitions that could potentially trigger old patterns of unhealthy thinking. This includes developing proactive strategies for managing predictable stressors, building resilience for handling unexpected challenges, and creating systems for recognizing when stress levels are becoming unmanageable. Peace I leave with you; my peace I give you. I do not give to you as the world gives. Do not let your hearts be troubled and do not be afraid. Many things will trouble us in life, but scriptures on mental health promise that we can find peace in Jesus.

Professional support may be needed periodically throughout your life as you face major transitions, traumatic events, or seasons when your usual practices aren't sufficient for maintaining mental wellness. There's no shame in seeking professional help when needed, and wise people recognize when additional support could prevent minor issues from becoming major problems. This might include periodic check-ins with a counselor, participation in support groups, or intensive therapy during particularly challenging seasons.

Environmental factors require ongoing attention because your surroundings significantly influence your mental state. This includes creating physical spaces that promote peace and reflection, limiting exposure to negative media or toxic content, and choosing activities and entertainment that support rather than undermine your mental health. Your environment should reinforce the healthy thinking patterns you've developed rather than constantly challenging them with negativity or chaos.

Lifestyle balance prevents the kind of chronic overwhelm that can gradually erode mental health even when individual stressors seem manageable. We have Jesus' example of taking breaks from the busyness of life to focus on spiritual matters, and He called His disciples to do the same. This includes maintaining appropriate boundaries between work and rest, scheduling regular times for recreation and relaxation, and ensuring that your life includes activities that bring joy, meaning, and spiritual refreshment.

Crisis planning prepares you for seasons when mental health challenges may return or intensify, providing clear steps to take when warning signs appear. This plan might include specific people to contact, professional resources to access, spiritual practices to intensify, and environmental changes to make. Having a plan removes the pressure of making good decisions during crisis moments and increases the likelihood of getting help quickly when needed.

Regular evaluation of your mental health practices ensures that your maintenance strategies remain effective as your life circumstances change and evolve. What worked during one season of life may need adjustment as you face new challenges, responsibilities, or opportunities. This ongoing assessment helps you stay proactive about mental health rather than reactive to problems that could have been prevented through earlier intervention.

Continuing to Grow and Evolve

Mental health recovery and spiritual growth are not static achievements but dynamic, lifelong journeys that offer continual opportunities for deeper healing, greater wisdom, and more complete transformation. The growth process, aka transformation requires participation. When we understand what the Biblical perspective is, Christians being followers of Christ, and the term "called to become Christ like" starts to get become clear and more reachable. This perspective transforms potential discouragement about ongoing challenges into excitement about continued growth possibilities and reframes setbacks as setup opportunities for deeper breakthrough rather than evidence of failure.

The concept of progressive sanctification provides a theological framework for understanding why growth continues throughout life rather than ending with initial healing or transformation. Just as physical development continues throughout various life stages, spiritual and emotional maturity unfolds over time through various experiences, challenges, and seasons of life. Getting realigned with God was the only way Jonah's depression could ever end, and this ongoing alignment process requires continuous growth in understanding God's character, His purposes for your life, and His ways of working in the world.

Embracing a growth mindset toward your mental health journey means viewing challenges as opportunities to develop new skills, setbacks as information about areas needing attention, and struggles as invitations to deeper dependence on God rather than evidence of personal inadequacy. This mindset shift creates resilience during difficult seasons and motivation for continued learning and development. It also prevents the perfectionist thinking that can create shame and discouragement when growth doesn't happen as quickly or smoothly as expected.

Deepening self-awareness becomes increasingly important as you mature in your mental health journey because greater awareness allows for more precise interventions and more effective growth strategies. This includes understanding your unique triggers, recognizing your personal stress signals, identifying your specific learning style, and knowing which spiritual practices and mental health tools work best for your personality and circumstances. This self-knowledge allows you to customize your growth approach rather than trying to force yourself into generic formulas.

Expanding your capacity for complexity involves learning to hold multiple truths simultaneously, tolerate ambiguity and uncertainty, and navigate situations that don't have clear-cut answers. Early in mental health recovery, black-and-white thinking often provides necessary structure and clarity. As you mature, however, developing the ability to handle nuance and complexity without becoming overwhelmed or paralyzed represents significant growth in emotional and spiritual maturity.

Developing wisdom involves learning to apply knowledge and principles effectively in real-life situations that don't always fit textbook examples. Biblical principles can help us find strength, hope, and resilience on our mental and emotional wholeness journey. The Bible offers profound wisdom and comfort in facing mental issues like depression, anxiety, fear, loneliness, stress, and grief. This includes discerning when to apply grace versus truth, knowing when to push through difficulties versus when to rest, and understanding how to adapt general principles to specific circumstances. Wisdom comes through experience, reflection, and ongoing relationship with God.

Building resilience involves developing the capacity to bounce back from setbacks, adapt to changing circumstances, and maintain your mental health foundation even during storms. This resilience isn't built through avoiding difficulties but through successfully navigating challenges with healthy tools and spiritual resources. Each challenge you overcome with healthy strategies builds confidence in your ability to handle future difficulties and increases your capacity for helping others facing similar struggles.

Expanding your ministry to others represents a natural progression in mental health growth as your own healing creates capacity and credibility for helping others. This doesn't necessarily mean formal ministry roles but rather the organic opportunities to encourage, support, and guide others who are struggling with issues you've successfully addressed. Your testimony becomes a tool for bringing hope to others, and your experience becomes a resource for practical guidance and spiritual encouragement.

Pursuing ongoing education keeps you growing in understanding about mental health, spiritual development, and personal growth rather than assuming you've learned everything you need to know. This might involve reading books, attending workshops, participating in support groups, or seeking additional counseling or spiritual direction. Continuous learning prevents stagnation and provides fresh insights and tools for continued growth.

Developing new areas of your life becomes possible as mental health creates the stability and energy needed for pursuing dreams, goals, and callings that were previously impossible. Mental health recovery often unlocks creativity, ambition, and vision that were suppressed during seasons of struggle. This expansion might involve career changes, creative pursuits, relationship improvements, or ministry opportunities that align with your growing sense of purpose and calling.

Regular life evaluation ensures that your growth remains intentional and directed rather than leaving development to chance. This involves periodic assessment of your goals, values, relationships, and spiritual condition to ensure that you're growing in directions that align with God's purposes for your life. These evaluations help you identify areas needing attention and celebrate progress in areas where you've experienced significant growth.

Embracing seasons of life acknowledges that growth looks different during various life stages and circumstances. The growth challenges of young adulthood differ from those of midlife or later years. Understanding and accepting these seasonal differences prevents unrealistic expectations and allows you to focus on the specific growth opportunities that each season provides rather than trying to force inappropriate goals for your current life stage.

Living as an Overcomer

The identity of an overcomer represents the culmination of your mental health journey—not because the journey ends, but because you now live from a fundamentally different understanding of who you are and what you're capable of achieving through Christ. Focusing on spirituality has helped many people in recovery from substance use disorders, and those with mental health conditions gain a more positive perspective that assists with their overall healing process. Living as an overcomer means operating from victory rather than struggling for victory, responding to challenges from strength rather than weakness, and approaching life's difficulties with confidence in God's faithfulness rather than fear of potential defeat.

The biblical foundation for overcomer identity is established throughout Scripture but perhaps most clearly articulated in 1 John 5:4: "For everyone born of God overcomes the world. This is the victory that has overcome the world, even our faith." This verse reveals that overcoming isn't based on personal strength, willpower, or circumstances but on the fact that you've been born of God and equipped with faith that transcends worldly challenges. Understanding this foundation prevents you from falling into performance-based thinking that measures your overcomer status by your current circumstances rather than your identity in Christ.

Overcoming mindset involves viewing every challenge as an opportunity to demonstrate God's power, every setback as a setup for a comeback, and every difficulty as a chance to grow in faith and resilience. This mindset doesn't deny the reality of problems or minimize their impact but rather approaches them with confidence that God will use even difficult circumstances for your good and His glory. God is our refuge and strength, an ever-present help in trouble. Therefore we will not fear, though the earth give way and the mountains fall into the heart of the sea. Scriptures on mental health are there to give us comfort and remind us that God is with us, even in those struggles.

Living proactively rather than reactively characterizes the overcomer lifestyle because you're no longer at the mercy of circumstances, emotions, or other people's actions. Instead, you make decisions based on your values, respond to situations based on biblical principles, and choose your attitudes based on truth rather than feelings. This proactive stance gives you tremendous power over your quality of life and prevents you from feeling like a victim of your circumstances.

Maintaining eternal perspective helps you evaluate temporary challenges in light of God's eternal purposes and promises. When you're living as an overcomer, current difficulties don't define your reality because you understand that this world is not your final destination and that God is working all things together for good. He will wipe every tear from their eyes. There will be no more death or mourning or crying or pain, for the old order of things has passed away. This perspective provides incredible stability during storms and prevents temporary setbacks from derailing your peace and joy.

Demonstrating kingdom values through your responses to adversity provides powerful testimony to God's transforming power and offers hope to others who are observing your life. When people see you responding to challenges with faith rather than fear, maintaining joy during difficulties, and choosing forgiveness over bitterness, they witness the reality of God's power to transform human nature. Your life becomes a living demonstration that the promises of Scripture are true and applicable to real-life situations.

Embracing your calling as a wounded healer allows you to use your experiences with mental health struggles to bring hope and healing to others facing similar battles. The Lord your God is with you, the Mighty Warrior who saves. He will take great delight in you; in His love He will no longer rebuke you, but will rejoice over you with singing. When we're battling our own mental health and mental illness, it often feels like we're going to a great war or battle alone, with no one beside us. Your testimony becomes a tool for encouraging others, your experience provides credibility for offering guidance, and your ongoing victory demonstrates that overcoming is possible for anyone willing to apply biblical principles and appropriate tools.

Building others up becomes a natural expression of overcomer living because you're no longer focused primarily on your own survival and recovery but have capacity and resources for investing in other people's growth and healing. This might involve formal mentoring relationships, informal encouragement and support, or simply modeling healthy responses to life's challenges. Your strength becomes a resource for strengthening others, and your peace becomes a gift you can offer to those still struggling.

Celebrating God's faithfulness becomes a regular practice that reinforces your overcomer identity and provides ongoing motivation for continued growth. When you regularly acknowledge God's goodness in your life, remember His faithfulness during past struggles, and testify to His power to transform difficult circumstances, you strengthen your own faith and encourage others to trust Him with their challenges. This celebration isn't based on circumstances but on God's unchanging character and proven track record in your life.

Walking in authority represents one of the most practical aspects of overcomer living because you learn to exercise the spiritual authority that God has given you over your thoughts, emotions, and responses to circumstances. This doesn't mean you can control everything that happens to you, but you can control how you interpret events, what you choose to focus on, and how you respond to challenges. This authority gives you tremendous power over your mental and emotional state regardless of external circumstances.

Living with purpose and destiny consciousness means understanding that your life has significant meaning and that your experiences—including your struggles with mental health—are part of God's plan to accomplish His purposes through you. This understanding transforms even difficult experiences from senseless suffering into meaningful preparation for future ministry and impact. Now may the Lord of peace himself give you peace at all times and in every way. The Lord be with all of you. Scriptures on mental health can give us peace in a time when we are feeling worried, anxious or scared.

The overcomer lifestyle isn't characterized by the absence of challenges but by the presence of God's power to handle whatever comes your way. You've learned that your thoughts can be tamed, your emotions can be managed, and your responses can reflect the character of Christ regardless of circumstances. This knowledge creates an unshakeable foundation for life that allows you to face the future with confidence, serve others from strength, and demonstrate to a watching world that God's power is available to transform any situation. Your new mind has indeed created the possibility for a completely new life—one that overflows with hope, radiates with peace, and impacts others with the transforming power of God's love and truth.

As you continue on this journey of mental renewal and spiritual growth, remember that you carry within you the mind of Christ, the peace that passes understanding, and the power to overcome any challenge through Him who strengthens you. Your transformation is complete enough to celebrate, ongoing enough to remain engaged, and powerful enough to change the world around you one thought, one response, and one day at a time.

CONCLUSION

The journey you've taken through these pages represents far more than acquiring new information or learning helpful techniques. You've embarked on a sacred transformation—one that Scripture promises is available to every believer who chooses to "be transformed by the renewing of your mind" (Romans 12:2). What began as a battle against destructive thought patterns has evolved into a complete renovation of your mental and spiritual landscape.

You now possess the tools to recognize lies disguised as truth, challenge negative thought spirals before they gain momentum, and replace fear-based thinking with faith-rooted perspectives. You've learned that emotions are signals rather than masters, that your past doesn't define your future, and that God's truth provides an unshakeable foundation for mental wellness. Most importantly, you've discovered that taming your thoughts isn't about perfection—it's about progression toward the mind of Christ.

The strategies you've learned—thought-catching, biblical meditation, cognitive restructuring, prayer-based processing, and truth declaration—are not temporary fixes but lifelong disciplines that will serve you through every season ahead. Your transformed thinking has already begun creating ripple effects in your relationships, decisions, and daily experiences. This is just the beginning.

As you continue forward, remember that setbacks don't erase progress, struggles don't disqualify you from victory, and questions don't diminish your faith. You are equipped, empowered, and eternally loved by the God who "has not given us a spirit of fear, but of power and of love and of sound mind" (2 Timothy 1:7).

Your tamed thoughts have become the foundation for an untamed life—one marked by freedom, purpose, and the unshakeable peace that comes from knowing whose you are. The mind of Christ is not a distant goal but a present reality. Walk in it, live from it, and watch as God uses your renewed thinking to transform not only your own life but the lives of everyone your story touches.

The battle for your mind has been won. Now live like the overcomer you are.

www.ingramcontent.com/pod-product-compliance
Lightning Source LLC
LaVergne TN
LVHW051543070426
835507LV00021B/2386